TO LILA:

Hope you ...

Kar...

20/4/18

BLUEY'S MAGICAL ADVENTURE

Enjoy the
Adventure,
imagine you are
there Sue Bingumshaw

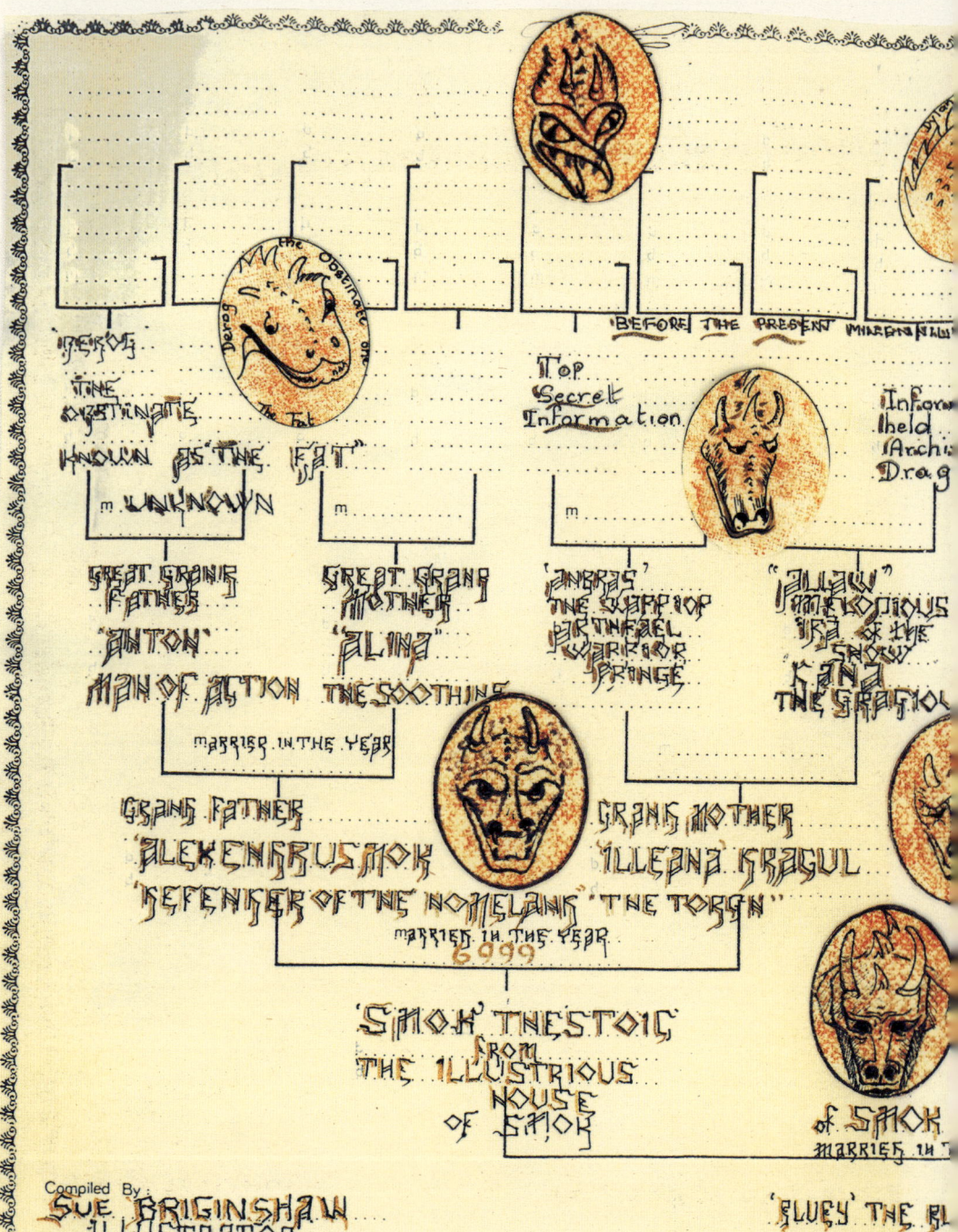

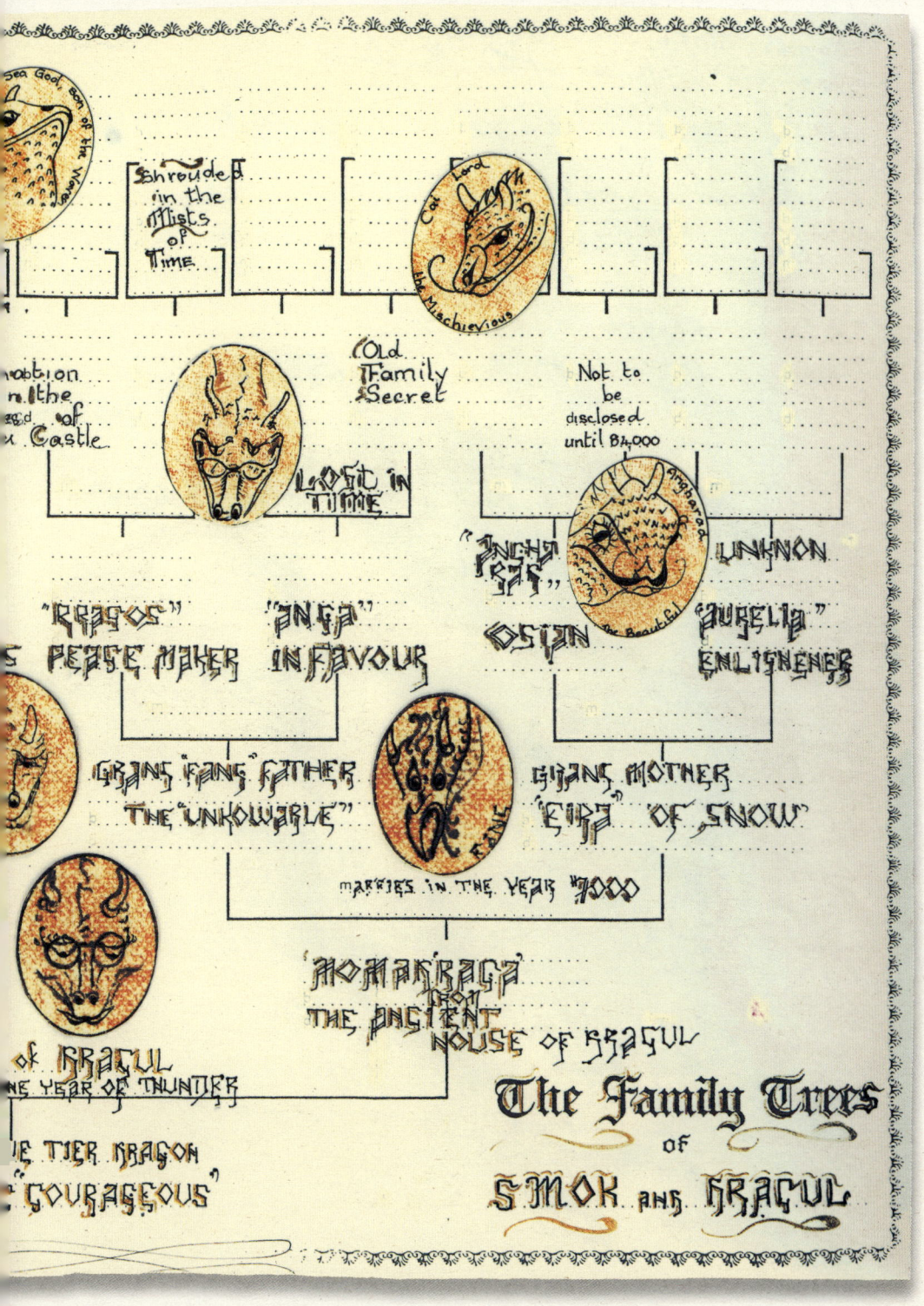

Bluey's
Magical Adventure

KEN MACKAY

ILLUSTRATED BY
SUE BRIGINSHAW

Contents

1	Bluey is lonely	Page 1
2	Dragon Mail	Page 10
3	Burney arrives	Page 15
4	Uncle Chin	Page 21
5	How to hunt for Snarks	Page 28
6	The Purple Possum	Page 38
7	The Garden's lair	Page 51
8	Fireguts	Page 56
9	Agbad	Page 64
10	Shock! Horror!	Page 75
11	What to do next?	Page 81
12	Getting ready	Page 93
13	Spells and potions	Page 108
14	Transylvania – Dragu	Page 125
15	Dragu's throne room	Page 141
16	Barry Basilisk	Page 156
17	Sebastian the Bold	Page 167

1
Bluey is lonely

Opening Spell
Orb, little Orb
You have travelled so far!
Zip Through the red heat of Dragon Fire
And icy cold of Black Night Air
Zip
Zip

Bluey was tired and feeling lonely. His tummy was hurting from eating too many sweet and sour gallnuts. Little, nasty-smelling, black smoke rings floated up from his nose each time he burped. He lay curled in one of Moma Draga's large golden wings as she snoozed in her favourite rocking chair by a red, roaring log fire. Her long whippy tail was carefully curled on one side of the chair, a half-eaten plate of gooberberry slices sitting by her feet.

 Before sunset, Moma had flapped home with minced Snark pie and gooberberry slices for dinner. As she prepared dinner, Bluey drooled as he watched her

super-hot, blue nose fire melt gobs of chocolate chips over the gooberberries. It was a yummy meal but Bluey felt unhappy despite a full rumbly, grumbly, burping tummy.

He looked up at Moma Draga's great yellow eyes and the wisps of white smoke coming out of her long golden nose. How happy he would be if there were another little dragon to go on adventures with every day, he thought. Sighing, he let out a puff of white steam and burped up a smelly black smoke ring again. Septimus, his dragon spider, snorted in disgust and retreated to the centre of his web by the fireplace.

Bluey decided to tell Moma about his day. He lifted himself up on one wing to be closer to Moma Draga's long pointy-head. Surely, if she hears how his day was, she would understand why he was feeling so unhappy. After all, it was months and months since Papa Smok had left on a sudden secret trip to see Auntie Burnice in far-off Transylvania.

Tapping Moma Draga gently on the nose with a sharp claw to wake her, he started his story. "Moma, after you flew off to the Purple Possum, I flapped over to the old goblin forest to find my friend Wart Nose. We splashed in the crystal blue pools and threw balls of goblin moss at each other. Then we played hide and seek in the forest. When we got

hungry, Wart Nose climbed on my back and I flew up to the Purple Possum."

Moma Draga chuckled. She worked as the head cook, and now she knew who had snitched the slices of Snark pie she had put on the windowsill to cool. Laughing, Bluey then told her what fun it had been to hear her thundering roar and see the jets of red fire spurt from her wide-open jaws when she had discovered that slices of pie were missing.

Moma laughed again at Bluey's story, particularly as Mrs P Hamster, fondly known as Mrs Pamster, had insisted on giving extra slices of Snark pie and gooberberry slices to Moma to bring home for Bluey. It was his favourite food. The gooberberry slices were a special treat for a hungry little dragon and his always-snacking dragon spider.

Then he told Moma that after their fun at the Purple Possum, Wart Nose had to go home to help his mum clean out their tree cave. Bluey flew Wart home. He then zoomed off to the great curved white sand beach at the Bay of Fires, but no one was there. So off he flew, up to the nearest mountaintop. All he did was frighten a large black bird who was feeding on the sweet and sour gallnuts hanging in the bushes. Feeling lonely, he quickly snacked on some then flew home to his lair, hopeful that Moma would be there. Arriving home, he found that the lair was empty.

Looking for someone to talk to, Bluey crept around the rugged cliff face towards his great Uncle Chin's lair. He told Moma, "As I came around the corner of the cliff, I heard a loud hissing and roaring. Poor Ping-Ling, Uncle Chin's magical Peng bird, was screeching with fright on a branch by the lair's door.

"Looking in, I saw Aunty Lulu throwing flying magic Chinese checkers at Uncle Chin as she shrieked that he had been cheating again! I then peeked through

the window and saw ivory white checkers flying around the room spurting red, green and gold flames as they flashed symbols while dodging jets of orange and blue flame that Uncle Chin was spitting at Aunty Lulu. She was furiously hissing clouds of steam putting out the flames.

"Oh, what a wild scene it was, as Uncle Chin kicked his tin leg on the rock floor like a great drum that jangled and boomed with every kick. I jumped back from the door, thinking it was a good idea to stay outside with Ping-Ling."

He went on, "What could I do? So, I decided to go see my friend Peter Pegasus."

And, that's what Bluey did. He flapped off around the mountain to a big broad valley covered in emerald green grass. There was a bubbling, crystal-clear brook running from a waterfall cascading from a high cliff. There, in the rays of the setting sun, he saw Peter prancing. His bronze hooves were sending orange sparks flying from rocks. He was also flexing his great golden wings, getting ready to go chasing stars across the black night sky.

Bluey circled carefully to land well clear of Peter's hooves. "Peter," he called, "can you play with me?" Peter paused, shook out his mane of long blond fur, and turned to Bluey. "Sorry little Bluey," he said in his booming voice, "the sun is setting and I have to fly off to chase the stars. They might get lost if I don't show them the right way to sail through the night sky. You should go home now or your Moma will worry." Peter spread his golden wings, leapt into the air, and with a *swoosh* disappeared into the sunset.

As he watched Peter's wings flapping into the distance, Bluey longed again to see Papa Smok's strong wings and hear him *swooshing* down to land after a day of Snark hunting. Bluey wished so much that his papa was home again. Then he had a sudden thought as he took off to fly home – why not drop by Barry Basilisk's den up by Skeleton Bay for a chat?

Barry was an ancient Basilisk who had come to live at Skeleton Bay near the Blue Tier from his home in Transylvania. He no longer spouted fire or froze creatures to stone with his fierce glare. He just loved to hunt Snarks and liked telling exciting stories to Bluey and his friends when they visited.

Bluey flapped down to land near the great red and grey stone dragon that marked the front of Barry's den at the edge of the cliff. Sure enough, he saw the huge black shape of Barry sitting on a rock gnawing on the remains of a Snark thigh. Bluey sidled up and tapped Barry's large knobbly knee with his pointy claw. "Well, well," rumbled Barry, "if it's not Mr Bluey himself. What a pleasure young man!" He smiled, showing his glowing amber eyes while flashing his bright blue serpent's tongue and chiselled black teeth. Bluey asked him to tell a story.

Barry laughed, telling Bluey that when Papa Smok got home there would be good stories galore. But, he added,

"It's time for little dragons to go home to their Momas. The sun is setting and the night is drawing near. Remember, little Bluey, in the night nasty things creep and crawl, so it's time for you to fly to your snug lair!"
Bluey sighed and did as he was told, flapping off towards the setting sun. As he circled down to land, a large shadow carrying a big wicker basket swirled in over his head. It was Moma Draga, home at last.

2
Dragon Mail

Thunk! *"Yee-ouch!"* yelped Bluey, as he woke up with a *thump* on the stone floor, the end of his tail in the fire. He whipped it out of the red-hot coals and rubbed the sleep from his eyes. There lay Moma Draga, sound asleep in front of the fireplace. She had opened her wings and dropped him! Curls of white smoke jetted out of her nose and spiralled towards the ceiling with each snore. One golden eye was slightly open.

He heard burbling, and turned to check on Septimus. Little puffs of fire were spurting from his nose. Septimus was laughing at him from his chain mail web hanging by the fireplace.

Before Bluey could creep off to his snug bed, he heard swishing and steaming noises in the chimney. He froze when he saw a bright red and gold-striped Orb

appear in the fireplace. It flashed blue sparks and let off jets of steam.

Dragon Mail! The Orb bobbed and bounced in the crackling flames, then zoomed out and hovered just above Moma Draga's nose. It let out a piercing whistle, sighed loudly, letting off more steam, and dropped, with a loud clunk, to the floor.

Moma Draga jerked awake and looked around to see what had startled her. "Bluey, what is happening?" Bluey pointed at the now silent Orb lying by the fire grate. "Well, well, Dragon Mail," Moma Draga cried. She hoped it was a message from her Smok. She snatched the Orb from the floor, turned it in her claws, and chanted an opening spell in Dragonish.

Opening Spell

Orb, little Orb, you have travelled so far,
Through the roaring heat of red dragon fire
AND icy cold blasts of black night air.
Now you are safe in a snug dragon lair,
So, pop off your top to deliver my mail!

The Orb shot out blue sparks, making a happy whistling sound. It flipped open to drop a grey-green Snarkskin parchment into Moma Draga's waiting claws.

She unrolled the crackling parchment. Bluey saw that it was covered in fiery red dragon words that danced and flickered in the firelight. Moma Draga hissed out a small jet of steam that calmed them down, and began to read.

"Why, Bluey, it's an urgent message from Aunt Burnice, all the way from Transylvania." Then, Bluey saw Moma Draga's face drop, and two pearly white tears appeared in her eyes as she read the words.

"Something terrible has happened," she gasped. "The evil Count Dragu and his black dragons are winning the fight against our golden dragons. Papa Smok has not been seen in weeks. Aunt Burnice is very worried about him. She also asks if she can send your cousin Burney to the safety of our lair as soon as possible. Once Burney is safe, Aunt Burnice wants to join the search for Papa Smok."

"How terrible! Poor Papa Smok," said Bluey. "But, I'd love to have cousin Burney come to stay. He can share my room."

Moma Draga dropped the Snarkskin parchment, and began pacing up and down in front of the fire. The fire seemed to crackle more with bright red and orange flames. Stopping and turning to Bluey she said, "Oh Bluey, I am so worried about your Papa! I must go to Burnice right now and I will bring Burney back to our lair."

Before Bluey could say anything, Moma Draga rushed off to her bedroom. Bluey heard lots of clattering and clanging. Moma Draga ran back into the room wearing her magic necklace of little red and black cooking pots; this had been given to her by Mrs P Hamster when Smok had left for Transylvania. Bluey saw them stirring and start to spout red and blue jets of flame. Moma's long golden head looked as though it was surrounded by a ring of flickering fire.

    Moma grabbed the Snarkskin parchment and let out another jet of steam. The fiery words disappeared. With the point of one claw she wrote a hurried note, sealing it with small jets of fire that she breathed over the parchment. She rolled it up, popped it into the Mail Orb and snapped on its top. She held the Orb tight and spurted a big jet of purple fire at it that made it steam and let off lots of blue sparks.

    Bluey heard her mutter a short spell in Dragonish and saw her throw the now brightly glowing Orb into the roaring fire. It twirled a few times in the flames, let out a shrill whistle, and disappeared up the chimney.

3
Burney arrives

Moma Draga flopped back into her rocking chair, closed her sad golden eyes and let out another spurt of swirling white steam. "Now we wait for Aunt Burnice to reply," she told Bluey. His head was spinning. He wondered why Moma Draga was so upset by the message? What had happened to Papa Smok? And why did Aunt Burnice want cousin Burney to come to the Blue Tier? What could he do to help?

Moma Draga sat silent as she waited, staring at the roaring red flames that leapt and danced in the fire grate. Bluey felt ignored, lonely and sad. He sat silently waiting for something to happen.

A small piece of gooberberry pie edging its way across the tiled floor got his attention. He stared at it, and looked again. Yes, the piece was moving; how? He saw a large red and black dragon spider clutching the edge of a piece of pie in two of its eight legs. Steam and little jets of yellow fire came out of its nose as it scrambled backwards towards its web by the fireplace.

Bluey chuckled; he should have known that Septimus could not resist a piece of gooberberry pie. He grabbed the pie from Septimus, who hissed like an angry tea kettle, and spat orange jets of fire at Bluey's armoured tummy. Bluey ignored him, and chomped the pie. Septimus climbed back into his web and sulked. Angrily, he blew smelly green and yellow smoke rings at Bluey.

Bluey had barely swallowed the gooberberry slice when he heard the whistling of the Dragon Mail Orb in the chimney again. This time, it jetted blue flames as it popped out of the fire. The Orb was glowing white hot from its long travels.

Moma Draga grabbed the glowing Orb and sang the Mail Opening song. Off popped its top and out fell a Snarkskin parchment. She held it up and read out loud the fiery words that shimmered and shook in her claw. It was from Burnice. "Come get Burney immediately and

I will tell you all that has happened! Come by Dragon Express – here is my magic landing symbol."

Bluey could see a swirl of green smoky fire in the middle of the parchment. Moma Draga grabbed a big black fire poker and put it in her mouth. She jetted orange and red flames until it turned red hot. She pulled it out of her mouth, then bent down and used the poker to draw a magic circle on the floor in flowing red and blue flames. In the middle she drew Burnice's landing symbol in green flames. They flared-up and smoke twisted towards the lair ceiling as if the flames were looking for a way to escape.

Moma Draga picked up her wicker basket, gave Bluey a quick kiss, and stepped into the middle of the circle. She hummed and swayed, chanting a spell. Her magic pots spurted multi-coloured flames – red, orange, blue, yellow and green – that looked like a cloud of fireworks exploding around her head.

As Bluey watched, a pitch-black cloud formed above Moma Draga, then slowly dropped down, covering her so that the jetting fires disappeared. Her humming grew louder and louder as the cloud pulsed and shrilled like a high wind whistling in the trees. Then, with a *FLOOMP, Floomp, floomp*, that echoed into the distance, the room was empty. The fires in the magic circle slowly flickered out except for a curl of green flame that continued to flicker towards the ceiling.

Bluey felt little iron spider feet dancing up and down on his shoulder. Septimus had seen the fires,

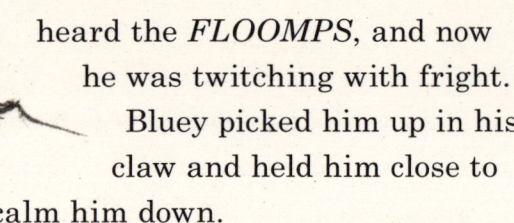

heard the *FLOOMPS*, and now he was twitching with fright. Bluey picked him up in his claw and held him close to calm him down.

"Don't worry, little gooberberry stealing spider, Moma Draga will be back soon." Septimus settled down and spun a short web of his best chain mail, hanging it from one of Bluey's ears, so that he could see what would happen next.

Bluey waited. He threw some logs on the fire and went into the kitchen to look for another snack. There, on the counter, was a wooden box where Bluey knew Moma Draga kept Purple Possum boysenberry tarts and gooey caramel slices. They were not as tasty as gooberberry slices in Bluey's opinion, but what was a hungry dragon to do? He opened the lid where fresh red and black boysenberry tarts were waiting to be chomped. Septimus jumped off his web and grabbed a piece of tart. "Greedy spider," Bluey yelled, and snatched up three tarts for himself before closing the lid. He went back to the fireplace and put Septimus back on his web so that Bluey could have his tart pieces. Septimus chomped his tart happily, but

even chomping tarts didn't stop Bluey worrying about Moma Draga and Papa Smok.

He wished he knew what was going on. He sat staring into the fire of leaping red and orange flames as he munched. He looked up on hearing Septimus's tiny chainmail links clatter and clang like little symbols and saw him shaking the web and stomping his iron shoes. Septimus was pointing to the fire. Bluey spun around. The magic circle was buzzing and glowed red again. Green and white smoke curled up from the pulsing landing symbol. A black cloud formed over the circle and bolts of yellow and blue lightening sizzled up and down its sides. A loud, weird, whistling started. Then with a very loud *FLOOMP*, the black cloud disappeared. There, standing in the middle of the circle holding her wicker basket, was Moma Draga!

The basket was covered in snow. It must have been cold and snowy in Transylvania, Bluey thought. Moma Draga stepped out of the circle and placed her wicker basket on the floor. The red flames and green smoke went out and the magic circle seemed to melt away. Moma Draga wrapped her arms around Bluey and hugged him. She bent down to open the lid of her basket. There, curled up in a ball with his golden wings folded tightly over his eyes, was a shivering, frightened, little dragon.

"Hooray, hooray," yelled Bluey in delight. "Burney is here!"

4
Uncle Chin

An excited Bluey blew smoke rings as he helped a shivering Burney climb out of the basket. He helped Burney over to the roaring log fire and sat him down to warm up. Moma Draga put her magic necklace away and headed into the kitchen to prepare a bedtime snack. Once Burney had warmed up, Bluey introduced him to Septimus. The dragon spider hissed his appreciation and blew orange smoke rings from the edge of his web. He was curious to meet another young dragon, one that had journeyed all the way from Transylvania to faraway Tasmania. Moma Draga returned with the remains of the boysenberry tarts from the wooden storage box.

After devouring the tarts Bluey showed a very tired Burney to his bedroom as Moma Draga made up the spare bunk bed. Promising Burney an exciting day exploring in the morning, Bluey fanned his orange ceiling glowworms to sleep with special cool green flames. Burney snuggled down into a warm bed, as the glowworms turned blue and winked out, leaving only the silver moonlight peeking into the room.

The boys woke with the golden sunrise. The smell of frying Burble bird eggs and sizzling slices of Snark skin wafted into the room. They soon joined Septimus in the kitchen and washed down breakfast with steaming mugs of Purple Possum spiced chocolate. In between burps, Bluey told Moma Draga that they were off to see Uncle Chin. Bluey, with Septimus on his shoulder, grabbed Burney by the claw and headed outside.

Burney scrambled to keep up with Bluey who was bouncing around the cliff to the next-door lair where Uncle Chin and Auntie Lulu lived. Bluey explained to Burney that Uncle Chin was a master of dragon magic, and one of the wisest dragons in the world. But, he warned, Uncle Chin also cheated at Chinese checkers. They reached the lair entrance and saw Ping-Ling sitting on his favourite branch, pecking at what looked like a strip of Snark thigh. Silver blue smoke curled out of an open window. Inside, two large dragons were shouting at each other.

Ping-Ling squawked a greeting and the shouting stopped. Bluey pulled Burney inside to introduce him to Uncle Chin who was leaning on the mantelpiece staring at Auntie Lulu. She was collecting terrified, quivering, Chinese checkers that were smoking hot and giving off golden sparks. Seeing the two young dragons Uncle Chin smiled and greeted them as if nothing had happened. Auntie Lulu offered the boys seats by the fire. Uncle Chin unscrewed his tin leg and settled into his large comfortable chair. Bluey then told them about Burney's sudden arrival. When he finished his story Auntie Lulu went into her kitchen to brew green tea and returned with a tray of piping hot Snark dumplings. Slices of golden dragon apple pie topped with creamy goblin ice cream followed.

 Septimus drooled at the sight of the apple pie and could not restrain himself. He snagged a piece from under Uncle Chin's nose. But before he could start munching it, Uncle Chin snorted, muttered a spell, and pointed a glittering golden claw at Septimus. The spider was flicked high in the air, but before he fell to the floor, red silken thread appeared. It twisted itself around his body so that Septimus hung in the air, hissing like an angry red and black beetle.

As Septimus struggled to free himself, the silk thread got thicker and thicker. His spider jets of orange flame could not burn the thread. Grinning, Uncle Chin closed his claw and poor Septimus fell to the floor bouncing like a red rag ball. The silken threads melted away as a very frightened Septimus scuttled up Bluey's golden blue scales to the safety of his flying harness.

Burney quietly dropped a piece of his pie behind Bluey. Septimus scuttled down, grabbed it, winked one of his eight red eyes at Burney, and retreated to his harness. Only Auntie Lulu noticed. She dropped a piece of Snark dumpling near Bluey on her way to the kitchen to clear up. Septimus wasted no time to grab and munch it. Soon contented spider snores came from Bluey's flying harness.

Before they left, Bluey plucked up the courage to ask Uncle Chin if he knew why Papa Smok was missing. Uncle Chin was about to speak when Auntie Lulu rushed over and whispered nervously into his ear. His great bushy eyebrows twitched up and down, giving off golden sparks of lightning, and small bolts of silver fire erupted from his nose. Bluey and Burney now knew something very serious was happening.

"Boys," Uncle Chin rumbled, "there are good things and bad things in the world. You both know how Snarks hunt and eat all sorts of animals and birds – well, there are evil things that hunt golden dragons, even Chinese dragons!" He paused and took a great gulp from an ornate

Chinese cup that had what looked like little golden Chinese dragons chasing each other around the rim. It was giving off swirls of yellow and green smoke.

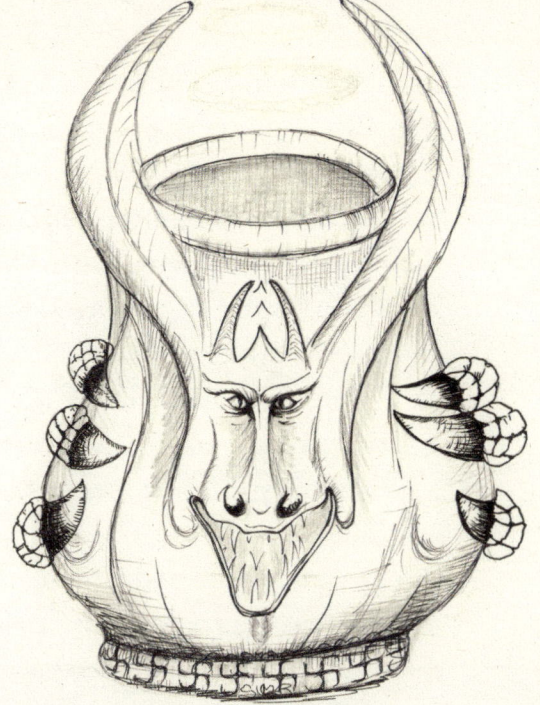

"Sadly, both Chinese dragons and golden dragons are being hunted down for their treasures. We came here from our ancestral lair in the great Moon Mountains of China to be safe from the terrible hunters. Bluey, your Moma and Papa came from Transylvania when you were only a baby, to be safe on the Blue Tier." Uncle Chin paused again, before going on. "The golden dragons, with help from their Chinese cousins, are now working together to hunt down the hunters. Bluey, your Papa Smok is one of the leaders of the golden dragons. Sadly, it will be some time before he can come home."

Bluey's heart sank, and he shivered with fear for his Papa. "But why did Burney have to come here?" he asked Uncle Chin.

"Here he is safe," Uncle Chin replied.

"But what about his mom, Burnice?" asked Bluey.

"Ah, boys, I can't say too much, except to tell you that Burnice is being well-cared-for while she helps the hunters."

Bluey, feeling more confident, asked, "And who are the hunters of golden dragons?" He just could not imagine anything or anyone who could harm a powerful golden dragon like Moma Draga or Papa Smok.

"Well," replied Uncle Chin, "many, many moons ago a dreadful creature called Dragu stalked Transylvania with an army of black dragons, even coming as far as China on their raids. They wanted the jewels and precious things that golden and Chinese dragons kept in their lairs. A fierce war was waged and Dragu and his army were defeated. Dragu was frozen into a block of ice by our friend Barry Basilisk and then buried under blocks of stone in a lair hidden in the Transylvanian mountains. We hoped he would never be seen again. But somehow Barry's spell has been broken and Dragu is on the march again, with a new army of ever-hungry Snarks and greedy black dragons!"

"Snarks and black dragons?" gasped Bluey and Burney in unison. "How terribly, horribly, awful!"

"Yes boys," said Uncle Chin, "It is terrible, but we are organizing and fighting back. Everyone on the Blue Tier is part of the resistance. Our dear old friend Barry Basilisk is on our side. Peter Pegasus is our chief scout. Mrs P Hamster and I are preparing powerful spells. Clever old goblin, Mrs K Bracken, will help with her shapeshifting skills. We have many ways of hunting with the help of some very strong spells and some secret powers that we only use when terrible danger comes." He grinned, "Now watch Auntie Lulu!"

He pointed his glittering claw, and murmured a Chinese spell. Holding her head high, Auntie Lulu smiled, and then dissolved into a great snowy sea eagle with shining black eyes and razor-sharp talons. Ping-Ling squawked and hopped into the room. He bowed low to the sea eagle, opened his own wings wide, and doubled in size. Flashes of green and gold light rippled through his feathers. Uncle Chin waggled his golden claw at Ping-Ling, who by now was the size of a full-grown dragon. He snapped his beak and hopped out of the room.

The boys were impressed. "So how can we help?" they wanted to know.

"Keep out of trouble and learn to be skilled Snark hunters." Uncle Chin answered. "You boys can help by being great Snark hunters right here on the Blue Tier."

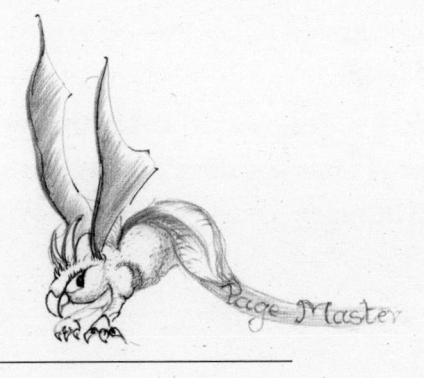

5
How to hunt for Snarks

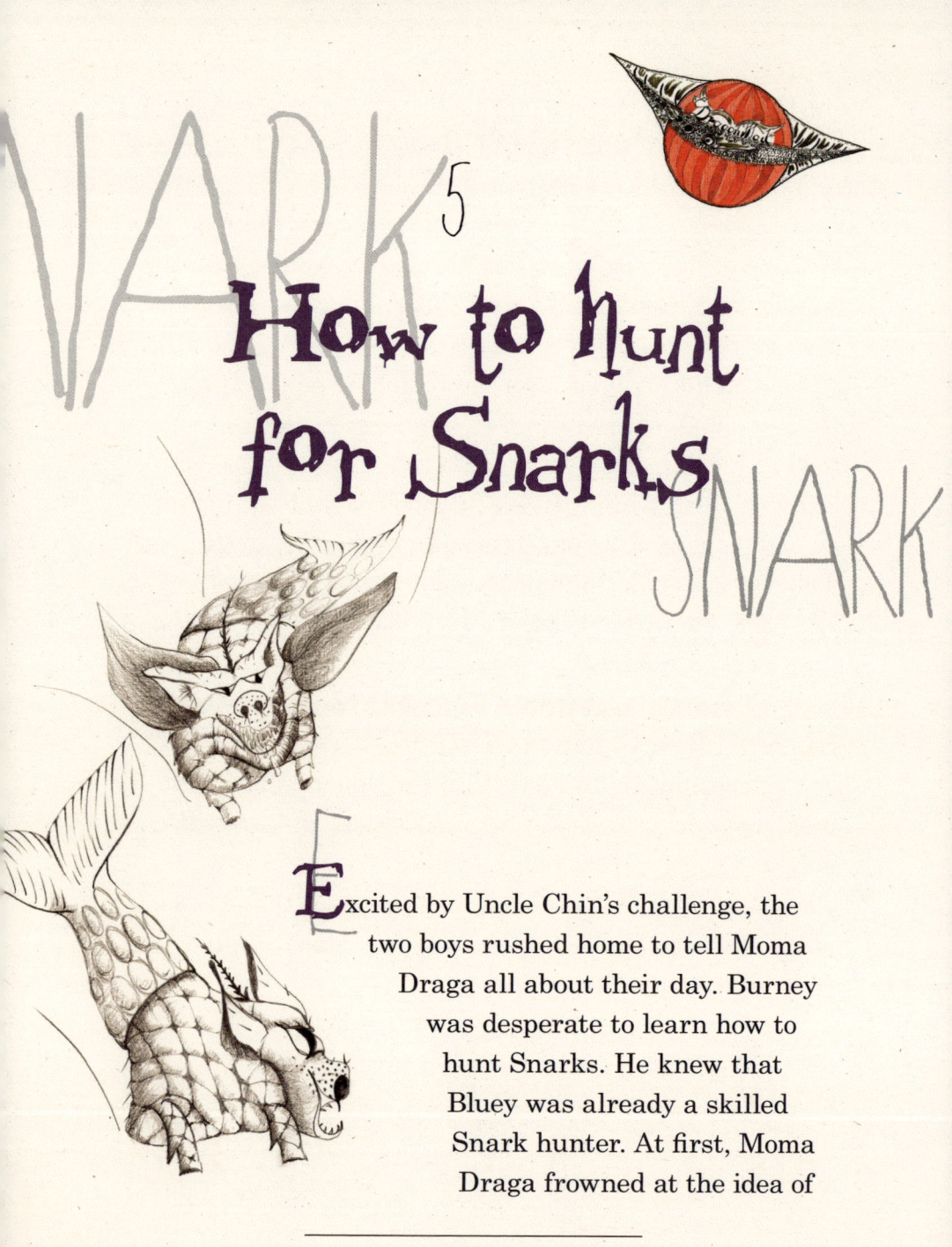

Excited by Uncle Chin's challenge, the two boys rushed home to tell Moma Draga all about their day. Burney was desperate to learn how to hunt Snarks. He knew that Bluey was already a skilled Snark hunter. At first, Moma Draga frowned at the idea of

Burney learning to hunt Snarks. It was dangerous for young dragons. But over a steaming meal of barbecue Snark thighs, followed by large slices of gooberberry pie, Moma Draga gave in. After all, she thought, Burney needed to join Bluey in Snark hunting, just as Uncle Chin had suggested. Turning to Burney, Moma Draga told him that first, before learning the art of Snark hunting, he had to get his own dragon spider.

Septimus, sitting on Bluey's shoulder as he did at meal times, carefully watched the boys with his eight ruby-red eyes, so that he could dart down to grab and chomp pieces of food that the boys dropped. But he was also listening carefully to Moma Draga explain what Burney needed to do.

After all, every dragon spider grows up learning about Snarks. They know that Snarks are like land sharks — about the size of a large wolf. They have grey and black armoured scales, long whippy shark-like tails, a short, sharp, black spike on their heads, and

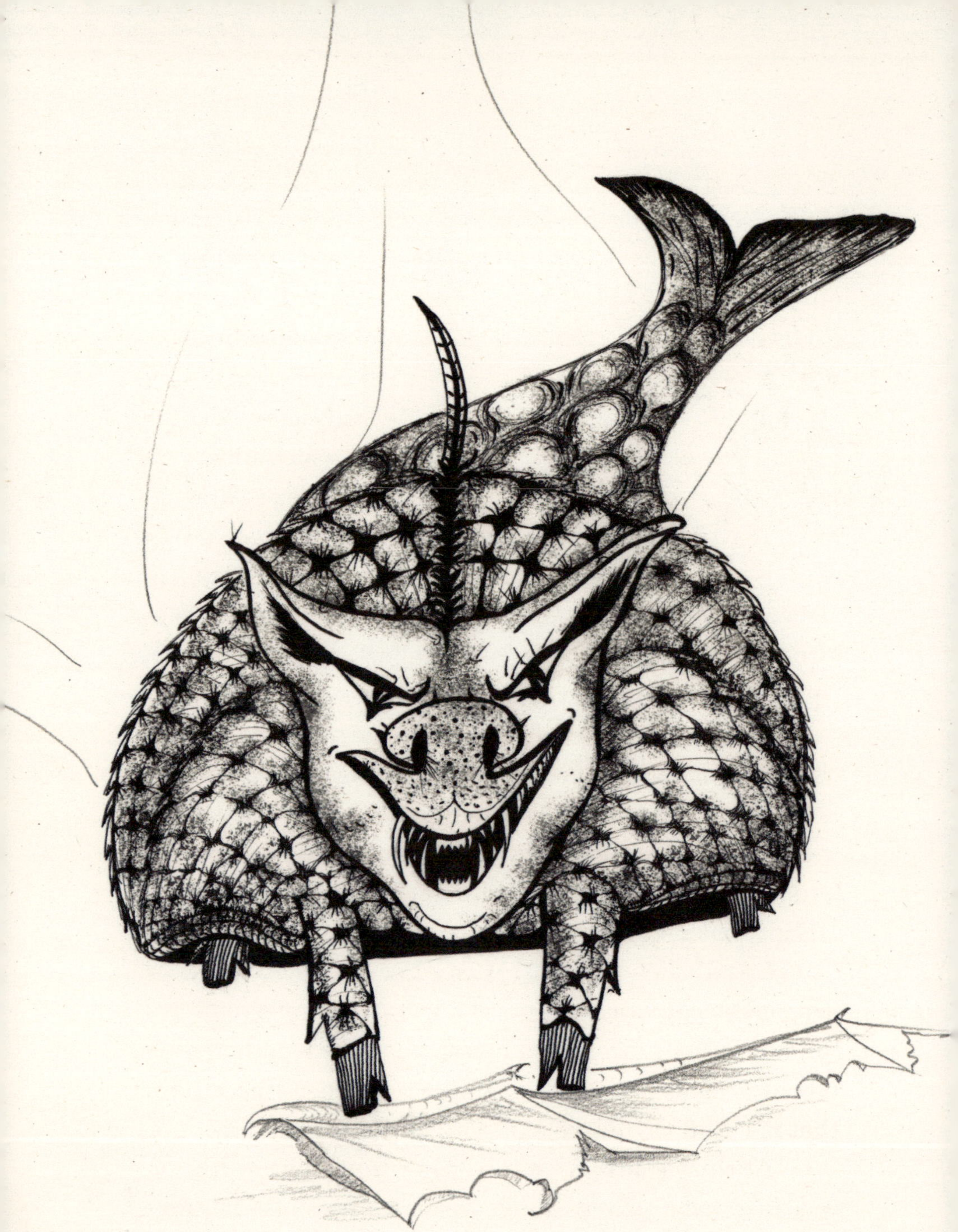

stubby black snouts with crunching-snapping razor-sharp teeth. Their large beady-red eyes always swivel around looking for food. On top of their heads are two pointy black ears that stand pricked up to catch the slightest sound.

Snarks like to eat all types of animals and birds; in fact, they will eat anything they can catch. Their only enemies are dragons and dragon spiders, because dragons are particularly fond of minced Snark pie sprinkled with pepper berries. Dragons also love snacks of steaming hot, fresh roasted, Snark legs.

Bursting with curiosity, Burney asked why dragon spiders were so important for hunting Snarks. Moma Draga explained that they were a special type of spider that had learnt to help dragons do their Snark hunting. She pointed to Septimus sitting on Bluey's shoulder, chomping on more gooberberry pie. "Look at him. His body is covered in chain mail scales studded with little sharp spikes. He has eight long red legs that allow him to jump and run very fast, and little iron shoes protect his feet. His multiple ruby-red eyes are on top of his head, so that he can look sideways or straight-ahead. Then, just like a dragon, he can breathe out coloured flame and steam from his twin noses. But most important, a dragon spider has two long fangs that, when he bites, can inject green poison that is lethal to Snarks."

At this, Septimus smiled at Burney to show his red, razor-sharp fangs. He let out a flair of bright orange flame followed by a whistle of steam while he chomped another piece of pie. He felt special, hearing Moma Draga describe him and how important dragon spiders were.

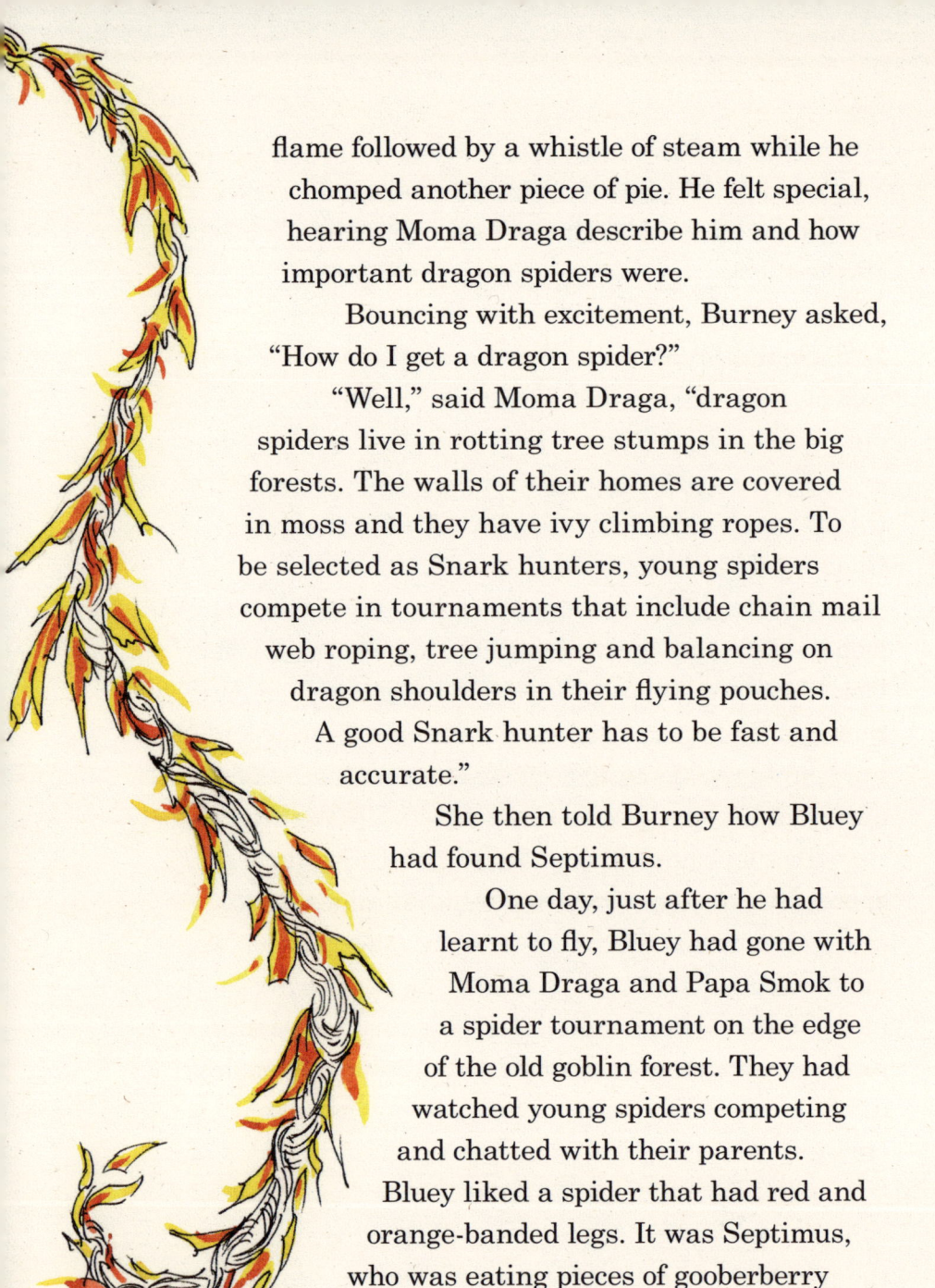

Bouncing with excitement, Burney asked, "How do I get a dragon spider?"

"Well," said Moma Draga, "dragon spiders live in rotting tree stumps in the big forests. The walls of their homes are covered in moss and they have ivy climbing ropes. To be selected as Snark hunters, young spiders compete in tournaments that include chain mail web roping, tree jumping and balancing on dragon shoulders in their flying pouches. A good Snark hunter has to be fast and accurate."

She then told Burney how Bluey had found Septimus.

One day, just after he had learnt to fly, Bluey had gone with Moma Draga and Papa Smok to a spider tournament on the edge of the old goblin forest. They had watched young spiders competing and chatted with their parents. Bluey liked a spider that had red and orange-banded legs. It was Septimus, who was eating pieces of gooberberry pie between events. Septimus soon spotted Bluey eating gooberberry pie and followed him around, picking up pieces of pie that he dropped.

Papa Smok thought Septimus would be a great hunter after watching him leap and loop his chain mail web around pieces of wood carved to look like Snark snouts. Moma Draga had agreed. Papa Smok asked Septimus's parents if he could be Bluey's hunting spider. They had both hooted in pride and arranged for Septimus to come and live with Bluey.

Burney then asked, "Why does Bluey have a special flying pouch for Septimus?" This time Bluey replied. "All dragon spiders have a special chain mail pouch with a little seat that is hung from a dragon's ear. This lets the spider talk to his dragon by tapping in dragon code on their ears. All dragon spiders learn dragon code as they grow up; the dragons talk by clicking their tongues."

"And Burney," Bluey added, "both the dragons and spiders use orange flying Orbs over their eyes which give them Shadow Vision. This means they can see Snarks hiding in bushes or behind trees in the forest. These Orbs look like the golden eyes of an adult dragon." Bluey turned and opened a box near the fireplace marked:

Snark Hunting Gear

in fiery red letters. Reaching inside, he pulled out a pair of flying Orbs and put them on.

The Orbs started to glow orange and then, with a high-pitched *zip-zip*, followed by another *zip-zip*, the centre of each Orb turned sky-blue and started to sweep from side to side. As they moved, the Orbs kept making high-pitched *zip-zip* sounds. Bluey turned and looked at the closed front door and directed Burney to look out the window. Bluey said, "With my Orbs, I can see a kookaburra sitting on the tree next to the door. Am I right?"

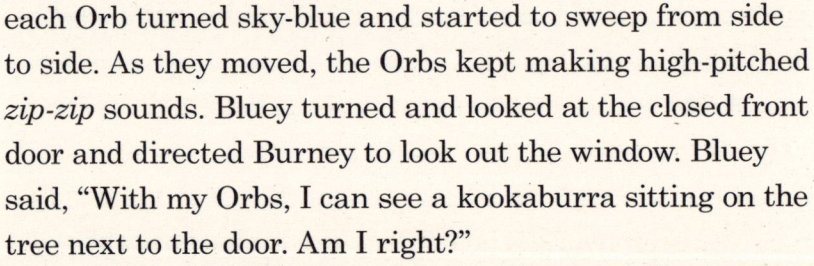

Sure enough, Burney could see the laughing bird sitting there. He was thrilled with the idea of having his own dragon spider, a pair of flying Orbs and learning to hunt Snarks.

Burney bounced up and down in excitement. "Wow, flying Orbs," he exclaimed. "When can I get a pair?"

"Not until you learn to hunt Snarks and learn to use dragon code," Moma Draga said.

"So, now tell me, how do you hunt the nasty snapping Snarks?" Burney demanded.

"It's teamwork," she replied. "The dragons fly to search for Snarks, each with his dragon spider in his flying pouch on his shoulder. When a Snark is spotted in the forest or bushes – Snarks are always close to somewhere in which they can hide – the hunting dragon swoops down as close as possible to where the Snark is, or where it's hiding. The dragon spider leaps off into a nearby tree or bush, ready to sneak up on the Snark. If he is lucky the dragon spider might jump straight onto the Snark's back. Septimus is very good at doing this."

Hearing Moma Draga's praise caused Septimus to let out a hoot of delight and he jingled his chain mail web so it hummed and clattered.

Moma Draga ignored him and continued, "As soon as the dragon spider lands on the Snark's back, he sinks his red fangs into it. It takes a few minutes for the deadly green venom to work. The spider then jumps onto the Snark's black snout and binds it up with loops of strong chain mail webbing. The Snark will buck into the air and howl in pain. The dragon spider leaps to the ground to watch and wait for the Snark to collapse in a heap of whirling tail and jerking legs. When it does, the brave dragon spider scuttles under the Snark and presses its red tickle button on the Snark's armoured belly. At this, the Snark dies laughing."

Burney laughed too, imagining the frenzied scene Mama Draga described. But he stopped when he saw Moma Draga frown at him. She wanted him to take her story seriously. She went on, "Finally, the exhausted dragon spider returns to his dragon. The dragon picks up the dead Snark in his claws and flies to the nearest Snark factory. There, the dragon spider is rewarded with as much gooberberry pie as he can eat."

At this, Septimus burped loudly, and scuttled around the boys' clawed feet looking for stray pieces of pie. Gooberberry pie is what a hungry dragon spider needs before bed to help him sleep.

It was past bedtime and the boys headed off to their bedroom, chatting excitedly about Snark hunting and their plan to search for a dragon spider for Burney. Septimus scuttled back to his warm web by the fire, chomping on a last piece of pie.

Moma Draga clattered plates in the kitchen as she cleaned up. She thought about how to help Burney find a dragon spider. She called out to the boys, "First thing in the morning we will visit Meff and Melie dragons in their lair by the Gardens at the end of the Far Valley. Septimus can ask Sam dragon spider when the next dragon spider tournament is to be held."

On hearing that, Burney bounced so high that he hit his head on the bedroom roof, scattering orange glowworms everywhere. After picking them up and sticking them back on the ceiling by their little sucker feet, the boys climbed into their beds. The glowworms turned blue and blinked out but Burney couldn't sleep. Every time he closed his eyes the words, "Hunt for Snarks, Hunt for Snarks," swirled around in his head, like black prickles on a gallnut bush. He tossed and turned and images of Uncle Chin's eyebrows shooting golden dragon sparks started to haunt him – the jumping sparks looking like Snarks running through tall grass. He knew from the snores coming from the other bed, that Bluey was already sound asleep!

6
The Purple Possum

Shafts of golden sunlight played on Burney's face as he woke up. What a week it had been! Specially that terrifying trip by Dragon Express in Moma Draga's great big wicker basket, all the way from his snug lair in Transylvania to her lair on the Blue Tier in Tasmania – a place he had heard about but never visited.

He remembered the sudden *FLOOMP* and flurry of blue and gold sparks when Moma Draga had arrived. She had greeted his mom, Burnice, with a huge hug.

PURPLE
Mystery Ingredients
Poison, not to be taken
HONEY DROP
DISSAPEARING CORDIAL
MAGIC CORDIAL
FUN CORDIAL
BURPING CORDIAL
SURPRISE CORDIAL
Syrup
Cordial
CORDIAL LIME
LEMON CORDIAL
FRIZZY CORDIAL
Magic Honey DROPS
MAGIC MUSHROOMS
ELIXIR
Add Bees Wings Water & Magic
Reference Book Honey Drops
The Purple Possum
1 2 3
Sale
Cash Register
Cash Draw
Management Mrs. Pamster
Flying Goggles
Snark Hunting Equipment Keep Locked
Magic Silver Rope

The two dragons had talked, for what seemed like hours, in an agitated way in the kitchen. Burney had stayed snug by the fire. Then his mom told him that he had to go and stay with his cousin Bluey for a while. Even more alarming, he had to leave with Moma Draga right now!

Without ado, Moma Draga had picked up the wicker basket, rushed outside and let out a huge cry in Dragonish. The rock walls of the lair rang with "Oh Smok, my Smok, please come home!" She rushed back in, covered in snow, and drew a magic circle and landing symbol on the floor. It had flamed red and given off green and white smoke. She then cast a Dragon Express spell, picked up Burney so he could give his mom a quick kiss, and shoved him into the big wicker basket, hissing, "Cover your eyes in your wings and don't open the lid until we land."

With that, there had been the snap and crackle of lightning – Burney could see the flashes through his closed eyes – and a great whistling and roaring of wind followed by the familiar *FLOOMP*. All he could feel was the basket twisting and twirling in Moma Draga's strong claw. Then came another loud *FLOOMP*, a sudden bump, and silence. Moma Draga had opened the basket lid and there stood cousin Bluey. Burney was so happy to see Bluey and to be on solid ground again, that the fright of his terrifying trip quickly faded.

 Moma Draga had offered Burney a big slice of gooberberry pie before showing him around their lair. Bluey introduced him to Septimus, who snitched a piece of fresh pie to munch. Burney had heard of dragon spiders, but had never met one, especially one who was famous for his Snark hunting skills. In Transylvania the golden dragons used large black ravens to help during Snark hunts.

    Rubbing his eyes, Burney was now ready for more adventures with Bluey. After a hot breakfast, Bluey and

Burney flapped over to the old goblin forest. They landed at the hidden goblin village to meet his friends, Wart Nose and George. Burney stared at them, as he had not seen goblins before. George was a shapeshifter goblin who delighted in adopting forms of ferocious creatures.

Bluey asked George to show Burney what shapeshifting looked like. Grinning, George's body flickered and switched into a snarling Tasmanian devil, then, in the wink of an eye, into a red-banded tiger snake. Finally he turned into a sharp-clawed sea eagle that took off and soared to the top of a nearby tree. Then, without warning, a small squeaking black bat landed on Burney's shoulder and started to munch on his ear. Burney yelped and swiped it away. The bat chirped with laughter as it turned back into George, who then hopped in delight around the amazed Burney.

Taking pity on Burney, Wart Nose, a tree goblin, offered to show him how, using his climbing ropes, he could swing between branches and leap from tree to tree. George and Bluey joined in. They played a tag game of hide and seek between shimmering silver pools of water, and threw orange, green and white balls

of goblin moss at each other. Becoming hungry, Bluey suggested they visit Moma Draga at the Purple Possum for a snack. George switched to monkey shape so he could sit on Burney's back between his wings and hold onto his neck. Wart Nose made a quick sling around Bluey's neck with his climbing ropes and sat next to Septimus who was in his flying pouch on Bluey's shoulder.

Bluey in the lead, they flew over the green valley up towards the inland mountains. Below, Burney saw a cascading waterfall and a silver river that ran down to the sea. The greens and blues of the eucalyptus trees painted the hillsides, punctuated by the browns of strange rock formations in which dragon lairs were hidden. When Bluey spotted the Purple Possum, he circled down to land. Burney landed next, and before he had folded his wings, Wart Nose, followed by George and a scuttling Septimus, had rushed in to see what goodies had been cooked that morning.

Ignoring them, Bluey whispered to Burney, "follow me," and he snuck around the corner of the building to the kitchen window at the back. There, sitting on the windowsill to cool, were freshly baked gooberberry pies. Drooling, Bluey ducked down and crawled across the lawn to the window. He reached up, but before he could grab a pie he felt a *WHACK!* Mrs P Hamster had hit his claw with a heavy wooden rolling pin. *"Yee ouch!!"* yelled Bluey. Standing behind her, he saw Wart Nose and George, with Septimus sitting on George's shoulder munching gooberberry pie. All three were laughing at him nursing his sore claw.

Moma Draga, who was carrying a small wicker basket, peered out from behind Mrs P Hamster. She chuckled too, at the sight of Bluey. She introduced Burney to Mrs P Hamster and said, "To avoid danger, he must stay close by Bluey." Mrs P Hamster stepped outside and hugged Bluey and shook Burney's claw. She told Burney that he was welcome at the Purple Possum any time. "There is powerful magic hidden here, so if you feel you are in danger, come straight to me. And now, come on in, have a look around, but no more snatching the goodies!"

She winked at Moma Draga, twirled around, and vanished in a puff of purple smoke. The boys and the young goblins stood there, staring pop-eyed at the spot where Mrs Hamster had been standing. There was no sign of her. They went into the living room. There, in the far corner they saw a strange claw-footed box bound by heavy silver chains. It was creaking and groaning as if something very strong was trying to get out. It was

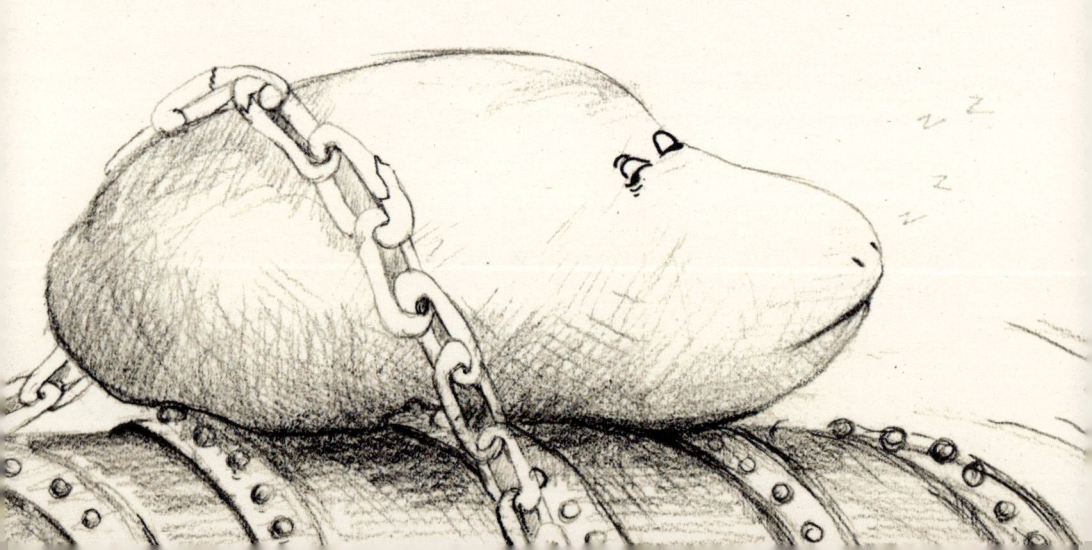

Mrs P Hamster's chest of powerful spells. Sitting on top, was a big rock with sharp beady eyes that swivelled to stare at the boys. At the sight of Moma Draga it whistled, made some grinding noises, closed its eyes, and started to snore.

    Moma Draga showed the boys around the shop and let them have more snacks, including a sample of her latest batch of minced Snark pies. She told them that they could deliver snacks to wise old Meff Dragon at the Garden's lair. Bluey was thrilled, because he enjoyed playing with her daughter, Melie Dragon, and her singing dragon spider, Sam. Septimus was keen to see Sam too, as he hoped he might teach him a song or two. He also liked to ride on the back of Whisky Dog, Melie's flying dragon dog. She had a pouch on her back for Whisky to sit in, when she was out flying or playing in the old goblin forest. She never took Whisky Snark hunting, though, because that was far too dangerous.

    It was mid-afternoon, so they decided to take the goblin boys back to their village on the way to the Far Valley. Bluey grabbed the small wicker basket in one of his claws. George turned himself back into a monkey, so he could cling to Burney's back, and Wart Nose clambered onto Bluey's back in his rope sling. They waved goodbye to Moma Draga, and headed for the goblin village. When they spotted the shimmering pools and multi-coloured goblin puffballs below, they circled down and the two goblins jumped to the ground. Wart Nose said goodbye,

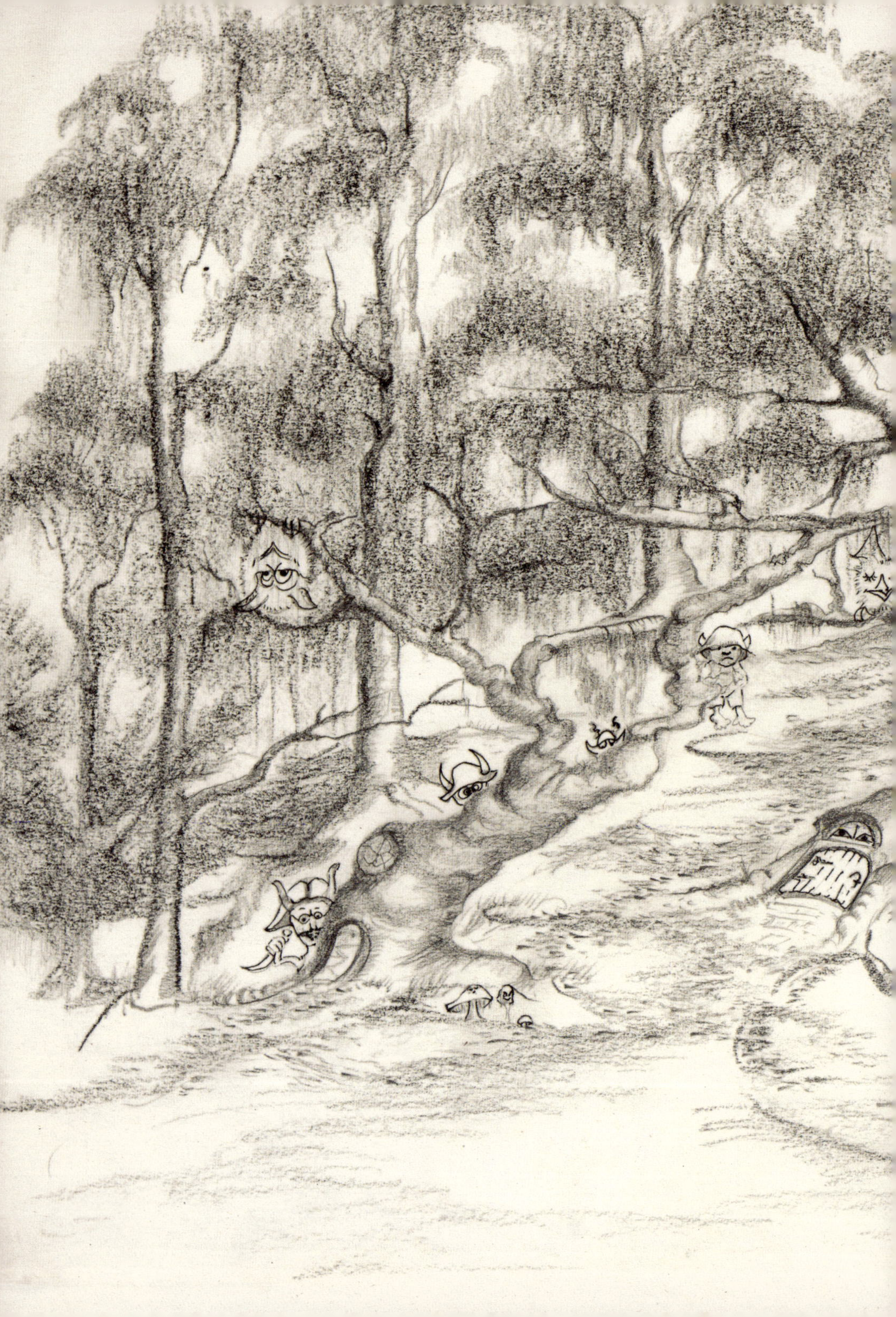

SMBRIGINSHAW

but George wanted to stay with the dragons. Bluey put down the wicker basket, and told George, "No," because they would not get back until sunset. George looked sad, but he ran off towards his tree house through the twisted forest trunks.

Bluey paused to pick up his basket before taking off. He told Burney that they had to fly fast as it was a long way to old Meff dragon's lair by the sea. The basket seemed much heavier. He noticed that it now had a garland of coloured goblin moss balls around its middle. How nice, he thought. "I wonder how they got there?" he said to Burney who had not seen them. "Anyway, Melie will like them," he said. They flew off, flapping high into the sky and headed towards the sea.

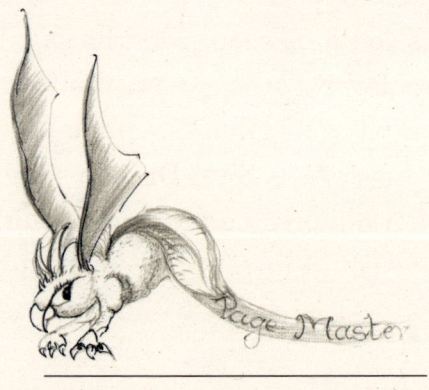

7
"The Garden's lair"

Sunlight danced over rivers and streams and cast shadows on the craggy cliffs as the two dragons flew towards the Gardens. Below them a broad valley headed towards the coast. Shimmering green grass lapped the blue sea. They reached the yellow sand dunes and saw a large heap of jagged, jumbled, rocks. Deep fissures and the openings of caves could be seen from the sky. Bluey circled down to land on a level platform near the top of the rocks. Melie dragon rushed out from a hidden doorway, followed by a bouncing Whisky Dog. Sam Dragon spider yodelled a welcome song from his perch on Melie's shoulder.

Before Bluey could introduce Burney, Septimus leapt down and scuttled over to Melie. Sam dropped to the ground and the spiders tapped their iron front feet in greeting, causing lots of little blue sparks to fly around. Whisky Dog sat and watched the spiders dancing, keeping a safe distance so that the orange flames and bursts of steam coming from the excited spiders didn't burn his nose.

Melie gave Bluey a friendly hug and welcomed Burney to the Garden's dragon lair. She asked Bluey why her favourite goblin friend, George, had not come. Bluey put down the wicker basket, but before he answered, they heard a loud goblin war-call from behind a nearby rock. George rushed out with a mischievous grin on his face.

"Oh, Bluey," he said, "it was such an effort to fly all that way from the old goblin forest to the Gardens, so we should open the basket and chomp the gooberberry pies your Moma has sent." Bluey and Burney were startled to see George. How had he managed to get to the Gardens?

Just then, they saw wise old Meff dragon circling above, preparing to land on the platform. She had spent the afternoon Snark hunting with her Dragon spider, Chomp, and she was tired and hungry. She removed her flying Orbs and picked up the wicker basket in her claw. She stopped, startled. She turned to Bluey and said, "Someone has used a strong shapeshifting spell on this basket!"

Bluey saw that the garland of goblin moss was gone. George held up a shaking hand and said, "I wanted to join the party and have some snacks!" Meff dragon raised herself to full height, let out a spurt of red flames and looking fiercely down at George, said, "You have a powerful gift in shapeshifting young George; keep it safe, keep it hidden, and use it only when you must. This is not something to play games with. You don't deserve a snack!"

Poor George! He had wanted to have fun with his friends at the Gardens and now he felt terrible. He hung his head in shame. Melie put a claw on his shoulder and said, "Oh, I am sure you only meant to have fun with us!" Bluey and Burney agreed. In the meantime Septimus had led the three dragon spiders to the wicker basket, which they had climbed. They were now trying to squeeze under the lid to get at the snacks. The sight caused everyone, including Meff, to laugh. Meff brushed aside the drooling spiders, taking care not to hurt them, and opened the lid. There was a wonderful feast of fresh minced Snark pies, golden slices of gooberberry pie, plus slices of boysenberry tarts, carefully put together by Moma Draga and Mrs P Hamster. Also, there stood bottles of the Purple Possum's famous cordial. It swirled and sparkled inside the glass, changing its colour to hues of orange, red, yellow and green and Mrs P Hamster's signature deep purple.

Everyone munched and chomped to their heart's content. Then Bluey asked Meff his all-important question. "Meff, can you tell us when the next dragon spider tournament is, as we have to get Burney a spider?" Meff looked hard at Burney and asked him, "Do you really want to learn Snark hunting? It's a very dangerous thing to do, you know!"

Burney was surprised to hear this. He knew that both Bluey and Melie were skilled Snark hunters who snared at least one Snark on each hunt. Bravely, he replied, "I want to join Bluey and Melie hunting horrible Snarks. My mum told me I had to learn how to hunt Snarks when she sent me here from Transylvania. Uncle Chin also told me I had to learn to be a Snark hunter." Meff replied, "Well, little Burney, the most important part of Snark hunting is the skill of your dragon spider. So, it is essential that we find you a very smart spider."

Chomp, Septimus and Sam had listened to this talk with great interest. They were huddled together, hissing to each other when Chomp suddenly scuttled all the way up Meff's body to her head, and tapped quickly in dragon code. Septimus and Sam watched, spurting jets of orange flames in excitement. "What is going on?" the three young dragons asked.

They saw Meff's eyes widen as Chomp tapped and then heard Meff rapidly click back to Chomp. She was saying, "Where does this spider live? Are you sure that his family would let him join a new dragon so soon?" Chomp tapped back, and Meff looked happy. "Well, we need to visit him at his home by the Red Fire Rocks, and find out if Burney and Jack dragon spider can team up as Snark hunters."

Septimus and Sam danced with excitement. They knew of Jack, and had heard what had happened to his great golden dragon, Fireguts, during a recent Snark hunt.

8
Fireguts

Before coming to live at the Fire Rocks on the Bay of Fires, Fireguts and his little brother, Burnbox, had been fierce fighters for the resistance in Transylvania. They had used their hot fires to clear away trees from the entrance to Dragu's castle so that the golden dragons could see who was coming and going. But as the fighting got worse, they had decided to move their families to the safety of the Red Rocks lair. From there, one dragon at a time volunteered to go back to help the resistance. It was Burnbox, who had volunteered to go back to Transylvania with Smok, leaving Fireguts at home.

 One cold, windy day, Fireguts, the biggest of the golden Fire Rocks dragons, had gone hunting. Jack, his dragon spider, had spotted a Snark galloping up the Fire Rocks beach. Fireguts adjusted his flying Orbs, and swooped down to give chase. But the Snark dived

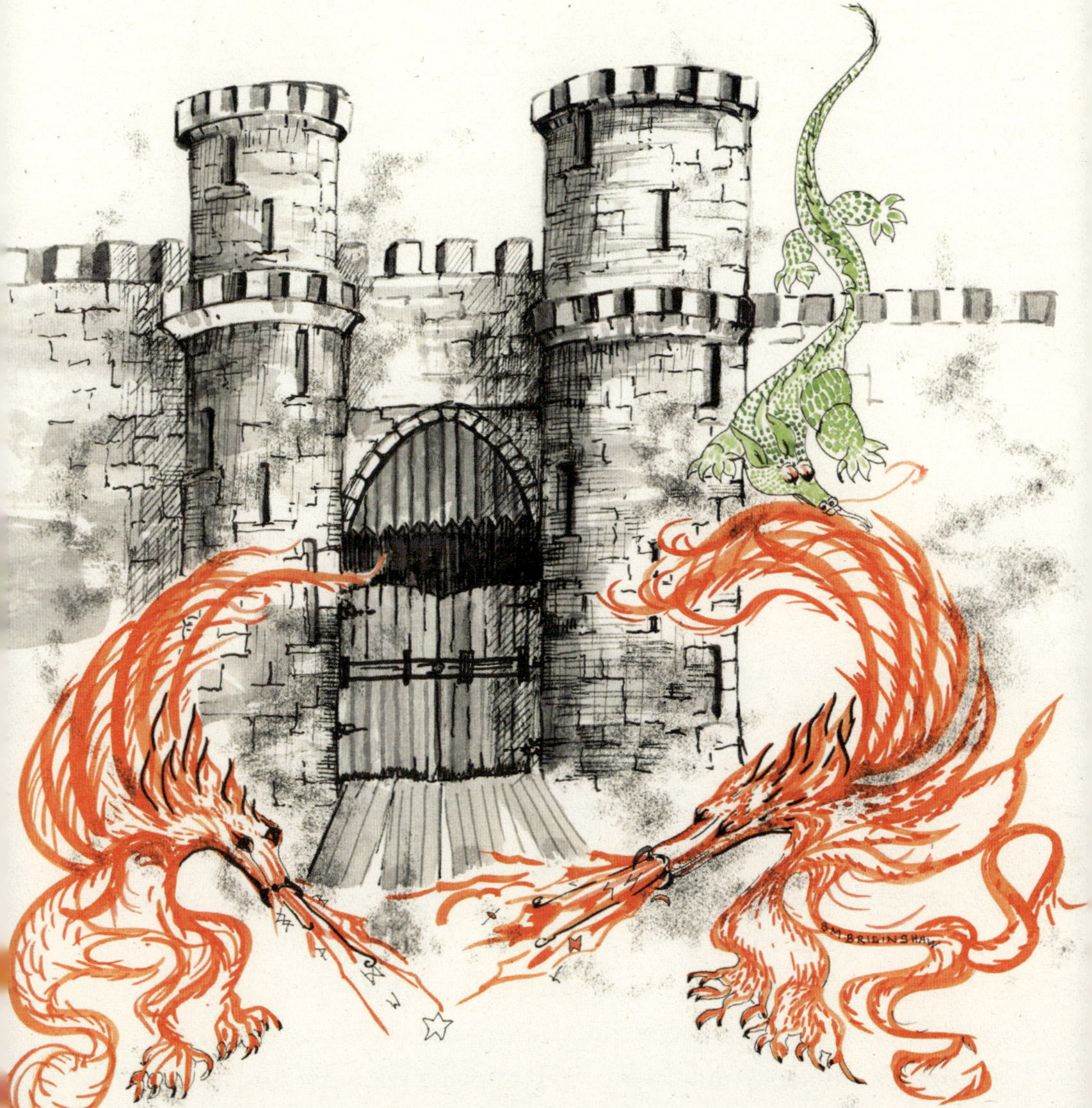

zit zit zit

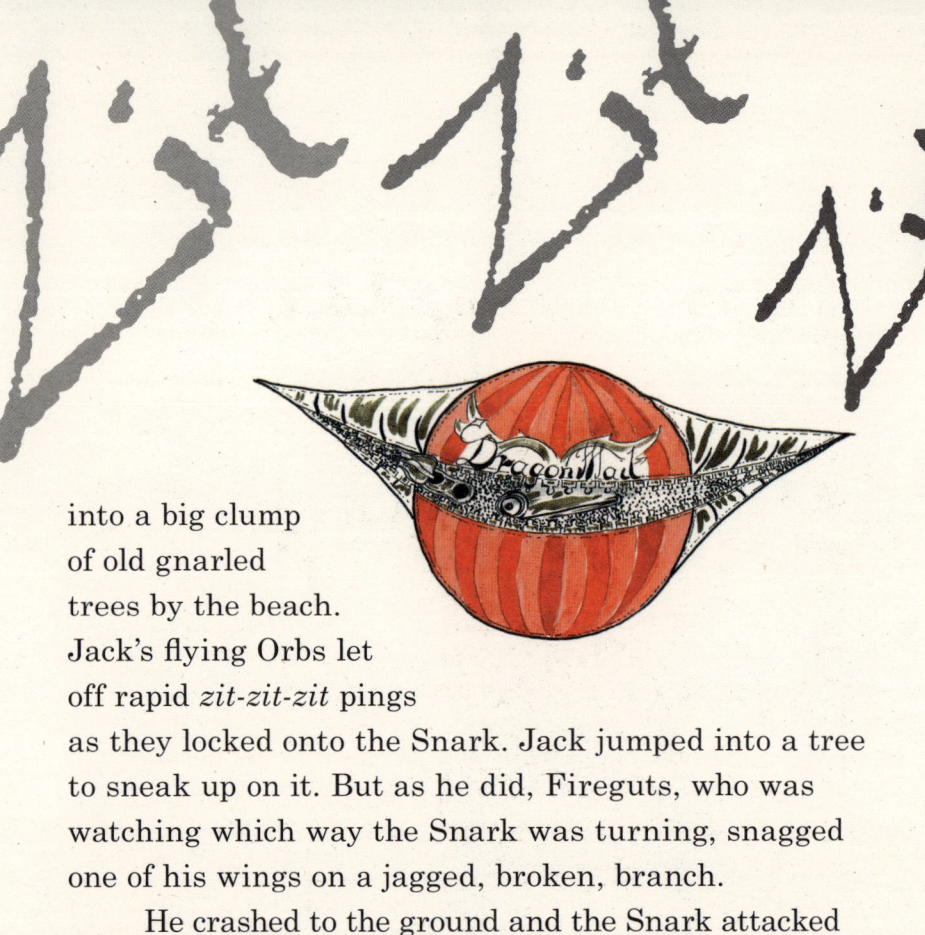

into a big clump
of old gnarled
trees by the beach.
Jack's flying Orbs let
off rapid *zit-zit-zit* pings
as they locked onto the Snark. Jack jumped into a tree
to sneak up on it. But as he did, Fireguts, who was
watching which way the Snark was turning, snagged
one of his wings on a jagged, broken, branch.

    He crashed to the ground and the Snark attacked
him. The snarling, howling Snark tried to rip and tear
at Fireguts's bloody wing, while Fireguts spurted red-hot
flames at the Snark, and kept spinning around to protect
his bleeding, torn wing.

    Horrified, Jack scuttled down and crept onto a low
branch of his tree, just above Fireguts and the Snark
who were twirling around and around in a terrible,
deadly dance. If Jack was to save Fireguts, he had to
jump very accurately and land on the Snark's back.
But getting a chance was difficult, because he had to

avoid being turned into a spider crisp by Fireguts's blasts of flames.

Speed was essential. The Snark would win if Fireguts tripped and fell over. Seeing Fireguts go under the branch, with the dancing, prancing, Snark close behind, Jack took a deep breath and leapt. Yes, it was a good leap! He landed on the middle of the Snark's back and sank his red fangs into its grey hide, and injected gobs of deadly green poison.

Jack had to work quickly, before the Snark could react to the burning pain in its back. He scuttled up the Snark's neck and looped a length of his silver chain mail web around the Snark's snorting snout. At this, the Snark let out a wailing, choking howl, and fell to the ground. Quick as a flash, Jack jumped off the Snark, rushed in, and pressed the Snark's red tickle button. The Snark curled up and died laughing.

Poor Fireguts collapsed to the ground, still holding his torn wing. He started to hum a magic healing spell and carefully blew special blue-green flames at the hole in his wing. His magical fire stopped his red blood from leaking out. But with an injured wing, Fireguts could not fly!

Help was needed. Jack scuttled up to the top of the nearest tree and anxiously spun a messenger web. He made a circle of silver chain mail with crisscross links made from a special type of chain mail that sang loudly when Jack twanged the links with his feet. "Help, help, dragon down," he twanged out in dragon code.

Mrs P Hamster, who had been looking for her favourite strawberries by the Fire Rocks meadows, heard the call. She pulled out her magic purple kerchief and waved it in the direction of the messenger web. With a flash of purple fire, she appeared by the dead Snark. Jack scuttled down from the tree to tell her what had happened.

She thanked Jack for his skilled kill of the Snark and then opened a small crystal bottle that swirled with red and green fires. From it she poured out purple ointment onto her kerchief and gently put it over the hole in Fireguts's wounded wing. The kerchief shimmered as it changed colour to match the golden scales of the wing. The hole disappeared, but a patched-up Fireguts still could not fly. She told him she would have to get the dragons at the Fire Rocks lair to come to his rescue.

Mrs P Hamster pulled another kerchief out of thin air, waved it, disappeared in a puff of purple smoke, and reappeared at Fireguts's lair. She told the dragons what had happened, and what they had to do.

Three great golden Fire Rocks dragons set off to rescue Fireguts, carrying a huge black chain mail sling. When they arrived, they dropped the sling next to Fireguts. One of the dragons picked up the dead Snark in his claws and flapped off to the nearest Snark factory.

Jack, who had been crooning soothing spider songs to Fireguts, stood clear to give the two other dragons room to spread out the sling. They carefully helped Fireguts climb onto it, keeping his injured wing by his side. They told Jack to hang on to his flying pouch that hung from Fireguts's ear, and they each grabbed an end of the sling and jumped into the air. They had to flap furiously just to take off.

As Jack flew with Fireguts back to the Fire Rocks lair, he thought how terrible it would be if Fireguts could not hunt Snarks again. He worried, "Where will I live if I don't have a Snark hunting dragon to look after me?"

When they arrived at the Fire Rocks lair, Fireguts was taken inside and laid gently in his favourite chair near the fire. A message spell was already writhing on the floor, sending green smoke up the chimney. With a flash of purple light Mrs P Hamster appeared clutching a large Snarkskin bag. It jangled and writhed in her paw. Without speaking, she rushed over to Fireguts, reached into her bag and pulled out a wand covered in silver stars that was singing to itself.

She chanted a healing spell in Dragonish as she put more purple ointment and green kerchief bandages on Fireguts's damaged wing. The other dragons stood by, their spiders on their shoulders, watching. But poor Jack had to stand on the arm of Fireguts's chair, dodging big gobs of purple ointment that dripped from Fireguts's wing.

When her work was finished, Mrs P Hamster put the wand back into her bag and told the waiting dragons, "Fireguts will fly again but not to hunt Snarks. I am sorry but his wing is too damaged for dangerous hunting."

Jack's legs buckled when he heard this, and he slumped to the floor with a small clang. Mrs P Hamster bent down and picked him up in her paw, which filled with a soothing purple light. As she held him, she looked at the dragons and said, "Brave Jack dragon spider saved Fireguts today, so please look after him and try to find him a new dragon to take him on Snark hunts." They all agreed, and promised to send out messages to the Blue Tier hunting dragons. Jack felt even better when Mrs Hamster produced a large slice of gooberberry pie, seemingly from behind her ear, and gave it to him as his treat for saving Fireguts from being ripped apart by the Snark.

Fireguts thanked Jack. He told him that he would send a message to wise old Meff dragon and her family in the Gardens. "Wait a while, and soon a new dragon will be found to take you on Snark hunts," he assured him.

Little did Jack know that it would be a young dragon called Burney who had yet to learn how to hunt Snarks!

FIGHTING DWARF 9
Agbad
AGBAD

The boys left Meff dragon and flew George back to the goblin forest, then headed back to their lair. They were bursting with excitement to tell Moma Draga that Jack dragon spider was to be asked to join Burney. Moma spurted golden flames when she heard the news. She was thrilled for Burney, because Jack was famous for his Snark hunting skills.

As the boys bounced around in the kitchen they chatted loudly about Burney learning to hunt Snarks. Moma prepared them a delicious late supper. After chomping down fried Snark thighs and slices of gooberberry pie they all went off to bed.

Burney snuggled down, thinking about his busy day. He watched the orange glowworms wriggle around on the ceiling, slowly turning to blue before they winked

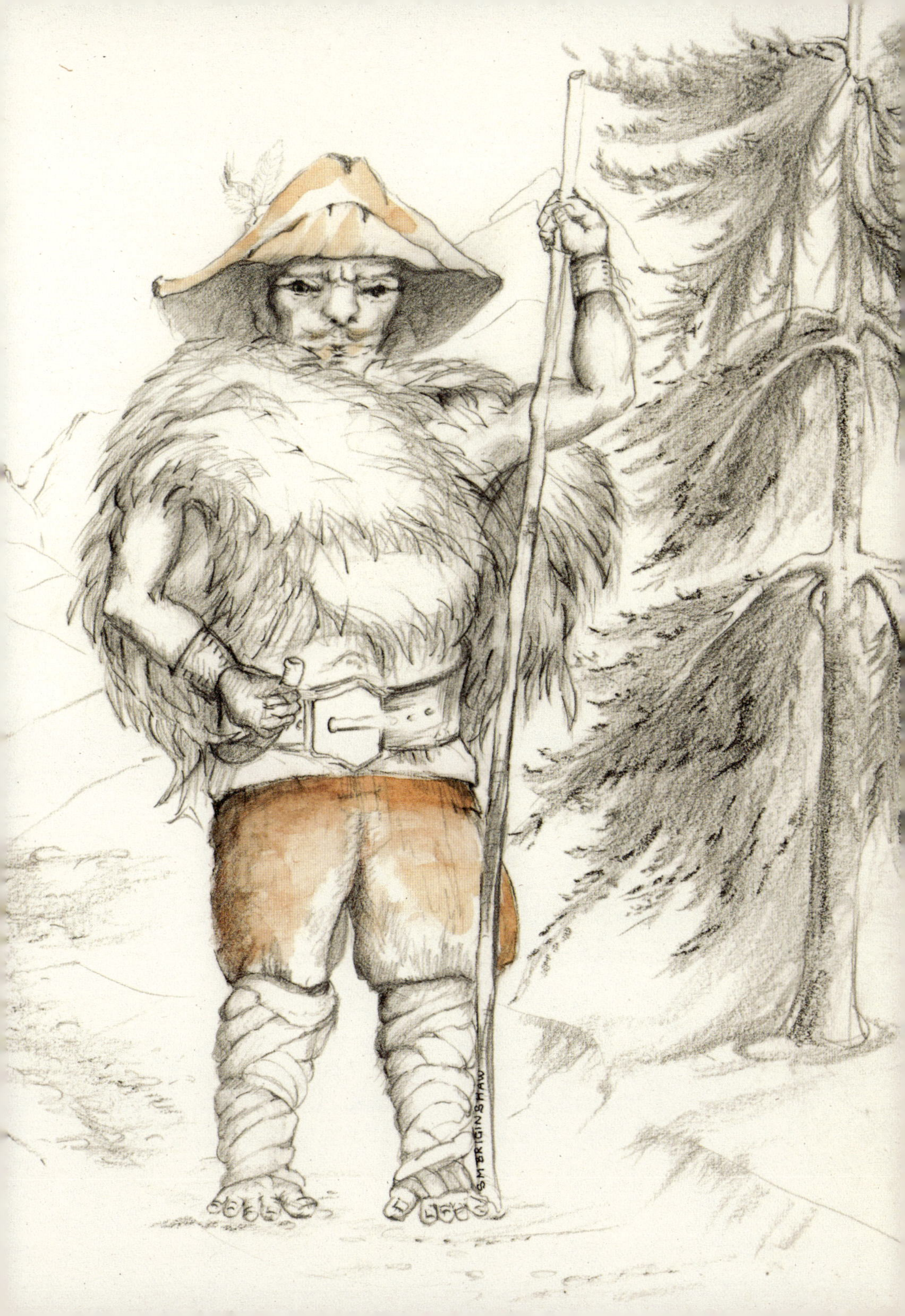
SM BRIGINSHAW

out. The room became dark, except for the faint cold-white starlight that came glimmering though the open window. The night was quiet, other than the crackle and pop of the dying fire in the living room, Bluey's snores and an occasional burp from Septimus.

As he lay awake, Burney heard the sharp crack of a twig breaking. He sat up and saw a yellow blob of light dart past the window. Sliding out of bed and quietly tiptoeing to the windowsill, he saw the blob of light creep towards the front door. Without waking Bluey, he slipped into the hallway. Startling him, he felt Septimus scuttle up his leg and onto his shoulder. Septimus tapped rapidly on his ear in dragon code, "Don't be afraid, it's a friend." Burney was very surprised; "How did Septimus know?" he wondered.

Judging by the loud snoring he heard coming from Moma Draga's bedroom, Burney decided she was sound asleep. As he snuck past, he saw that she had one golden eye slightly open. He crept down the hallway to the massive front door. It was made of black oak beams reinforced with iron bars to keep the lair safe. It even had a strong locking spell to protect it from being opened by strangers. Smok had cast the spell before he left for Transylvania. Only dragons living in the lair could open the door. Yet, as Burney watched wide-eyed, the door groaned and started to swing open.

Into the hallway stepped a hooded figure, lit up by a yellow blob of light. Burney was frightened. He was about to yell out to Moma Draga when Septimus grabbed his ear and tapped, "Wait, wait." Burney now saw that the cloaked figure carried a brown travel pack. Seeing

Burney, the figure stopped, put down the travel pack, and leant a gnarled walking staff against the wall. It had a group of yellow glowworms wrapped around its end.

The figure threw back its brown cloak to reveal a young fighting dwarf carrying a quiver of black javelins. He had two matching razor-sharp scimitars sticking out from each side of his broad leather belt. The glittering scimitars seemed to be alive, covered in writhing runes of purple fire. A wide-brimmed furry hat covered his head.

Bowing to Burney he whispered, "I am Agbad! You must be Bluey. I have come at Smok's order to meet a young dragon called Burney who is going to learn how to hunt Snarks. But first I need to give Moma Draga some very urgent news!"

Before Burney could reply, there was a loud thump from Moma Draga's room as she leapt out of bed. She rushed out, spouting golden flames, and fell upon Agbad with open wings, as if she wanted to crush him. But instead, Burney saw that she was hugging him in joy.

"Agbad, Agbad, how wonderful to see you," she cried. "How did you travel all the way from Transylvania? How is my Smok? Tell me all," she demanded.

Agbad staggered out of Moma Draga's embrace, and said, "Yes, of course. But first, I must call the members of the resistance here, so everyone can hear my news."

A sleepy, bleary-eyed Bluey, stumbled into the hallway. He wanted to know what the commotion was all about. Septimus leapt onto Agbad's shoulder and scuttled under his hat. Agbad turned and bowed to Bluey, introducing himself as a close friend of Smok's, who was helping the resistance in Transylvania. Moma Draga quickly interrupted, pointed to Burney, and explained that he was the one who had to learn how to hunt Snarks."

They all moved to the living room, where Moma Draga stoked up the log fire, and went to the kitchen to produce another plate of gooberberry pie. They now had to wait for the others to arrive, so they could hear Agbad's story.

Bluey was wondering how the resistance members knew to come to the lair when the fire suddenly flared. As if waiting for this moment Agbad pulled out his scimitars and carefully crossed them on the stone floor. He reached into the fire, grabbed a burning branch, and with a quick flourish, drew a black circle around the scimitars. Their purple fires joined together jetting towards the ceiling glowworms. He then reached into his leather pouch and pulled out a black leather bag that glittered with silver stars. Opening its neck, Agbad sprinkled a sparkling white powder onto the pulsing jet of purple fire.

With a loud boom, like a bronze Chinese gong being hit with a metal hammer, the purple fire split, changing into three bright red stars that flickered and bobbed near the ceiling.

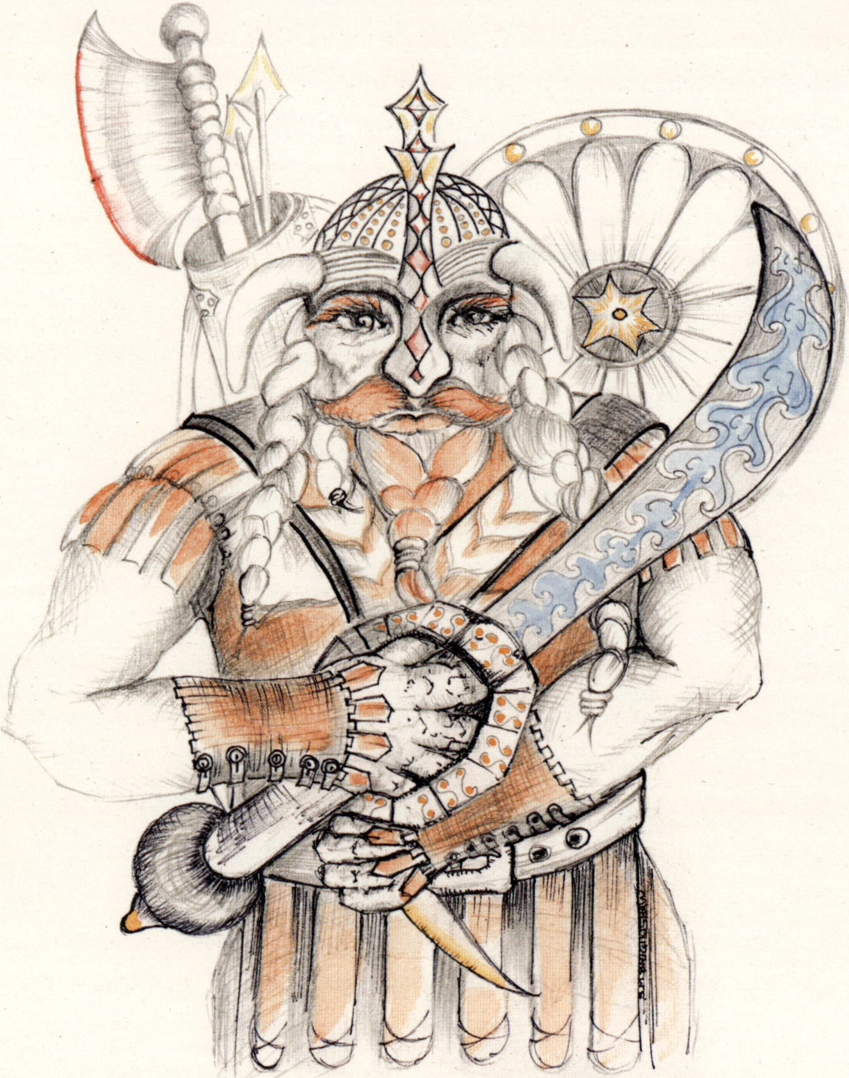

Reaching down with both hands Agbad grabbed his scimitars. He whirled the scimitars over his head so they started to buzz and hum with magic power. Bringing them crashing down together in an almighty

C-c-clang!!!

Agbad let out a piercing wail, like a black banshee being spitted on a javelin. Echoing Agbad's wail, the red stars whirled faster and faster around the room as if looking for a way out. Swirling into the fire with a loud *swoosh*, they whirled up the chimney, vanishing into the dark night.

Agbad slumped back into his chair. Bluey saw a tear creeping down his tattooed cheek. Moma Draga, who had sat frozen in her chair while Agbad summoned the messenger stars, stared at Agbad with a worried expression on her face. Bluey and Burney who had stopped chomping while Agbad made his fire circle, stared at the two of them, waiting for someone to speak. Agbad sat stone-still, breathing hard, saying nothing. Then Bluey saw that Agbad's hat was twitching.

A small, pointy, dragon-like face appeared over Agbad's left ear. The creature crept down onto Agbad's ear and let out an annoyed hiss. "A dragon lizard?" thought Bluey. It appeared annoyed at not being given a snack. Before anyone moved, Septimus scuttled out, grabbed the lizard by the tail, and pulled it back under the hat. The twitching stopped. Still, Agbad said nothing.

Burney leant over and poked Bluey. He whispered, "Can you hear those wings?" Bluey could hear the *swoosh, swoosh* of massive wings, then a mighty *thump*. A huge creature landed outside the front door. The door crashed open, and in came Barry Basilisk carrying a big black leather pouch. He rushed over to Agbad, hugged him, dropped his pouch to the floor with a *clang*, and sat down facing Moma Draga. He ignored Bluey and Burney. Not a word was said.

The fire suddenly glittered with silver flames; a golden glow grew in the grate and quickly turned into a golden globe. It rolled out of the fire onto the floor. Then expanded and expanded again, like a balloon being blown up. The globe split in two and out stepped Uncle Chin and Aunty Lulu. Ping-Ling was sitting on Uncle Chin's shoulder, his beady red eyes glittering.

Bluey and Burney watched bug-eyed, as the Chinese dragons rushed over to Agbad and hugged him. Uncle Chin's eyebrow lightening flashed like silver daggers and his hollow leg clanged, changing colours like a crazy kaleidoscope, as the spells inside tried to get out. The Chins sat down facing Moma Draga and, like Barry Basilisk, ignored the boys. No one spoke.

A wind sprang up outside, and whistled in the trees. The yellow moon disappeared behind thickening black clouds. Still, no one spoke. Then, the front door groaned open again, and a purple cloud of smoke writhed in. It hovered between Barry Basilisk and the Chins for a moment, let out a sibilant sigh, and vanished. There stood Mrs P Hamster, her whiskers flashing purple fires. She rushed over to Agbad, knocking off his hat as she hugged him. There, on his head, was the wriggling dragon lizard being held down by Septimus, and Snap, Agbad's dragon spider. Mrs P Hamster froze, pointed at the lizard, and asked Agbad why he had this strange creature.

    The silence in the room broken, Agbad's serious look changed to a laugh. He reached up and gently picked the dragon lizard off his head. "This is Frizzy Lizzy, a frilled lizard. She hates Snarks, and she is my spy. She speaks dragon code, and she is an expert at hiding from the enemy."

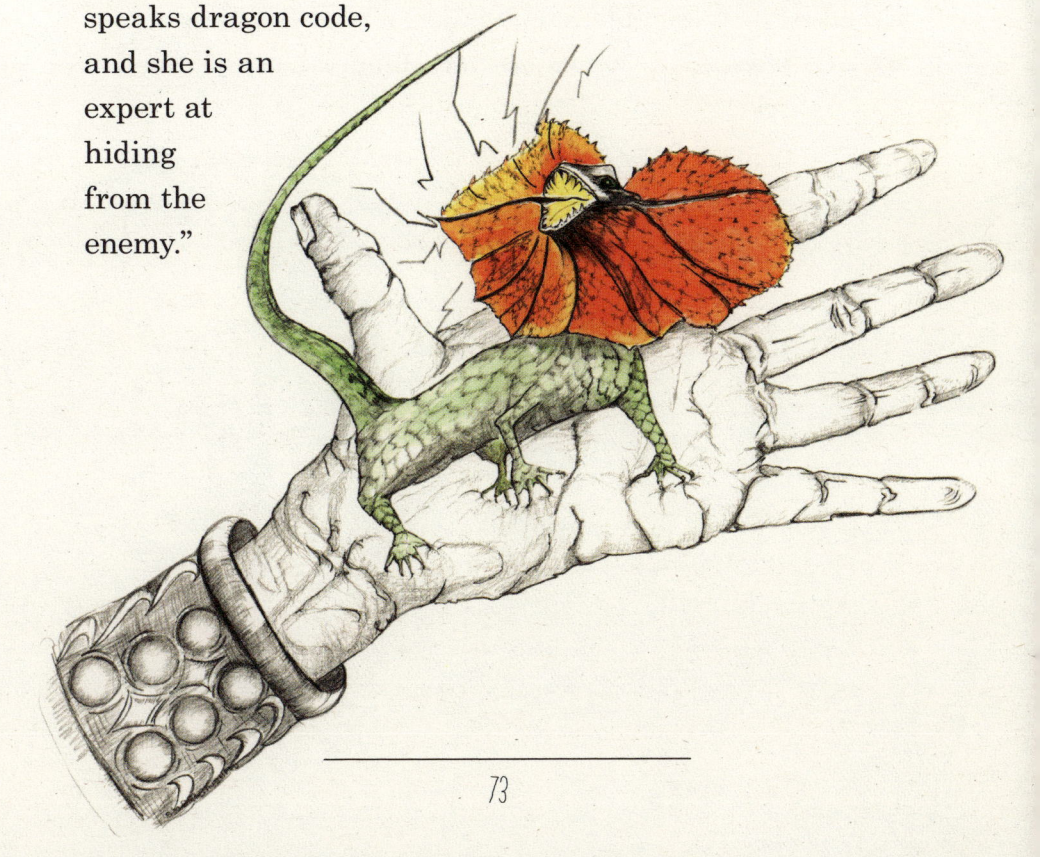

Looking at the lizard sitting in his hand, he commanded, "Frizzy. Go hide." Frizzy scuttled down to the floor, and ran over to a wall of the lair that was studded with little stalagmites. She started to climb. Agbad clapped his hands and, startling Bluey, Burney and Septimus, Frizzy disappeared. Mrs P Hamster smiled. She walked over to the wall and pointed to a stick-like stalagmite. It was Frizzy in her frozen position. Everyone clapped at Frizzy's skill.

"And, she's hungry," added Agbad, "She loves gooberberry pie and of course minced Snark pie." Bluey responded to the hint and handed a bit of pie to Frizzy. Agbad nodded his appreciation, declaring, "No more tricks, I'm ready to tell you my story."

10

Shock! Horror!

The fire was stoked again. More gooberberry slices and minced Snark pies were put out, as everyone settled back into their chairs. Taking a deep breath, Agbad began to speak.

"With Peter Pegasus's help I came as fast as I could. Terrible, terrible things have been happening in Transylvania. Dragu's army of black dragons and Snarks has got stronger. The local resistance is crumbling as more prisoners are taken and our fighters die in battle. Only a few golden dragons remain. All the Chinese dragons have gone." Ping-Ling let out a bone-chilling screech on hearing this horrible news.

"But much, much, worse, Smok has been captured by Dragu and turned to stone! He stands in the throne room of Dragu's castle with his wings outstretched as if to fly back home."

At that shocking news Moma Draga, jetting red flames, leapt out of her chair and let out a loud wailing cry, then crashed to the floor in a faint. The room echoed to her wails and some of the glowworms fell off the ceiling, making the room darker. Everyone except Uncle Chin rushed over to help her up. He was frantically unscrewing his hollow leg to get out a special magic spell. The horrified boys sat frozen in their chairs. They could not lift an adult dragon, especially a big golden dragon like Moma Draga.

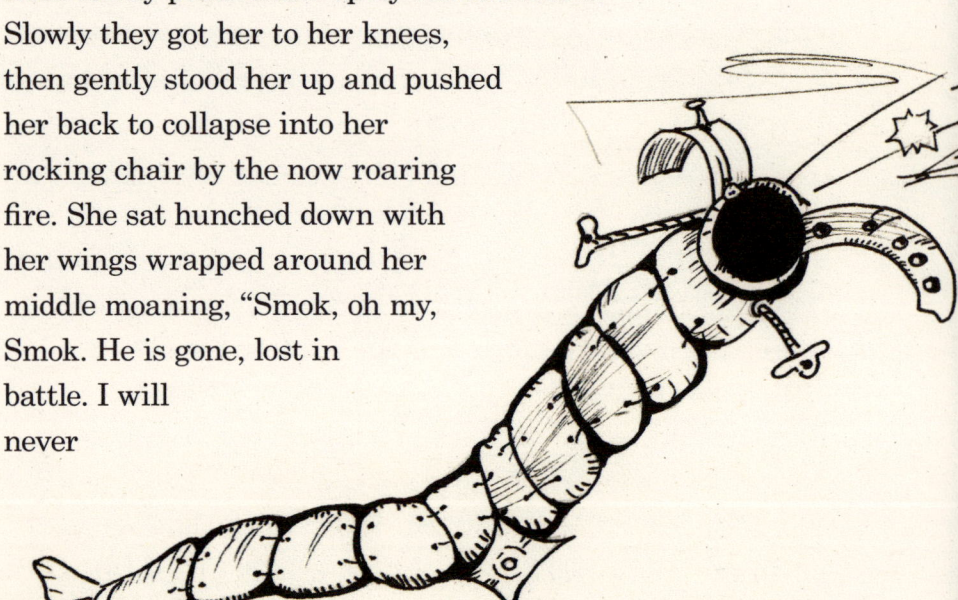

But lift her, the others did. Mrs P Hamster gently held Moma's head in her paws as Barry Basilisk and Aunty Lulu slowly pushed her up by the shoulders. Slowly they got her to her knees, then gently stood her up and pushed her back to collapse into her rocking chair by the now roaring fire. She sat hunched down with her wings wrapped around her middle moaning, "Smok, oh my, Smok. He is gone, lost in battle. I will never see him again! What will I do now? Oh, Smok, how could this happen?" Moma Draga's great head fell forward, and the boys saw big pearls of tears oozing out of her golden eyes. Her breathing was ragged and only little jets of steam were coming out of her nose.

Mrs P Hamster pulled a large purple kerchief out of her pouch, stretched up, and began to sing a high-pitched, healing song as she gently wiped away Moma Draga's tears.

Suddenly, with a shrill shout, Uncle Chin pulled out of his hollow leg an odd-looking rock that was rapidly changing colours – black to blue, red to orange, green to yellow – while it shot out little silver sparks. "Hee Wah Yah Ping! This is it," Uncle Chin shouted at the top of his voice. "Sprinkle powder from this rock on Smok and he will be transformed." Ping-Ling crowed loudly and danced a jig on his shoulder.

Everyone stopped to stare at Uncle Chin and his strange rock.

Only Barry Basilisk spoke.

"I am sorry, but my spell to protect Smok

is far too strong to be broken by that little rock. I gave Smok a powerful Basilisk spell to protect himself from Dragu before he left for Transylvania. It was only to be used as a last resort if Dragu captured him. Cleary that is what he has done and turned himself into stone." Everyone looked at Barry in shock and horror at what his spell had done to Smok. Barry thundered on, "We Basilisks have the most powerful magic in the world to turn any living creature to stone!"

Mrs P Hamster spoke up, "But surely if your spell can turn Smok to stone you can reverse it?" "Yes, indeed I can," said Barry, "but it requires my presence to cast the spell." They all gasped and started to talk at once, asking, "How do we get a Basilisk into Dragu's throne room?"

"It's impossible," said Uncle Chin, "We have to use the powder from my rock."

"No," Barry thundered, "Didn't you hear me? My magic is far too strong."

By now Uncle Chin's eyebrow lightning was threatening to jump off the top of his head. It crackled and sparked around his ears and ran up and down his nose. He pointed to Frizzy Lizzy where she remained motionless on the wall and said, "Let us test these spells. Barry, you freeze Frizzy into stone and I will try powder from my rock to bring her back to life."

Agbad let out a yell, "But what if you fail? Poor Frizzy will just be a piece of rock!"

Mrs P Hamster stepped away from where Moma Draga was now snoring quietly in her rocking chair, her soothing spell having taken effect, and said, "I agree with Uncle Chin. It's worth trying, as getting a Basilisk into Dragu's throne room is an enormous challenge!"

Barry stood up to his full height. The boys shrank back as he towered over everyone. They could see his jet-black eyes gleaming like bottomless black pits as they swirled with powerful magic. He stomped over to the wall where poor Frizzy remained frozen with fear, and gently tapped her on the head saying, "Don't worry little lizard, you won't be hurt. You won't even remember what happened."

In fright, Frizzy twitched and began to scuttle down the wall, heading towards the safety of Agbad's hat, which was still lying on the floor. But before she had moved more than a few paces, Barry stretched out his big arm and pointed a black claw at Frizzy. Red-black fire leapt from the end of his claw and curled around her head. She froze, mid stride, looking just like a rock lizard carved out of the wall.

Barry turned, sat down again and said, "Now Uncle Chin, please release our poor little rock Frizzy."

Quickly Uncle Chin produced a small bowl plus a sharp silver grater from his hollow leg. He held the sparking rock over the bowl and grated off some flakes. They sparkled and hissed like fire coals in the rain. He tapped the edge of one of his eyes, causing silvery drops of water to fly out. He caught and mixed them into the flakes of rock. The bowl began to smoke and flicker with blue flames. Leaning on Aunty Lulu, he limped over to the wall. Chanting a spell, he dipped a silver claw into the bowl and splashed some of the blue flickering liquid onto Frizzy's head. It smoked, flickered out and dripped down the wall. Nothing happened.

Agbad now frantic, yelled, "You said she would not be hurt! She is still frozen!"

Uncle Chin shook his head and tried again. Still nothing happened. Sighing, he sat down in defeat.

Barry got up and stomped over to the wall. He lifted his great clawed hand and once again red-black fire ran from his outstretched claw to curl around Frizzy. As if nothing had happened, she hissed, twitched, and finished her scuttling run to Agbad's hat.

Everyone clapped and yelled in excitement. Maybe there was a way to save Smok, after all. But how do you get a Basilisk into Dragu's throne room?

11
What to do next?

Moma Draga opened her eyes. She saw Mrs P Hamster, Uncle Chin, Aunty Lulu, Agbad and Barry Basilisk, sitting in a circle talking quietly. The two boys were asleep in their chairs. Septimus, Snap, and Frizzy Lizzy were chomping gooberberry slices. The fire was glowing softly in the grate. Why was everything so calm? She didn't feel calm; she felt shocked and very sad. Her Smok was trapped, frozen into stone in Dragu's throne room. She sobbed quietly, splashing big pearls of golden tears on to the floor.

A chair scraped, and a furry paw holding a purple kerchief that pulsed with various shades of purple, gently wiped away Moma's tears. Mrs P Hamster's face was frowning in anger, yet her big green eyes glinted with pity, as she leaned closer to Moma Draga. She whispered, "Don't you worry, my special friend. We have a plan!" She waved her free paw, calling the others over to Moma Draga's rocking chair.

Uncle Chin, who had screwed his leg back on, clanked over. The noise woke Bluey and Burney. Agbad strode over to Moma Draga, and Barry Basilisk following, stomped across. Aunty Lulu seemed to glide through the air. The dragon spiders, scuttled over to gather on Septimus's web by the fire. Frizzy Lizzy scampered up to the mantelpiece, grabbing another slice of gooberberry pie on the way. She pretended to be a piece of grey-black stick while she snacked, dropping crumbs for the spiders.

Everyone watched Moma Draga. Uncle Chin rumbled, clearing his throat to speak, but Moma Draga spoke first. "Oh, my Smok," she cried again, "How do we know he has not been smashed into a pile of stones by that terrible Dragu?" She began to cry again, more golden tears splashing to the floor. Mrs P Hamster wiped them away with her pulsing purple kerchief. Bluey was frightened and sad for his Papa Smok, but, noticing that the kerchief was dry, wondered where were the flood of tears going? Seeing his puzzled look Mrs P Hamster explained that golden dragon tears could be used to make very strong spells, so she kept them in a silver flask at the Purple Possum.

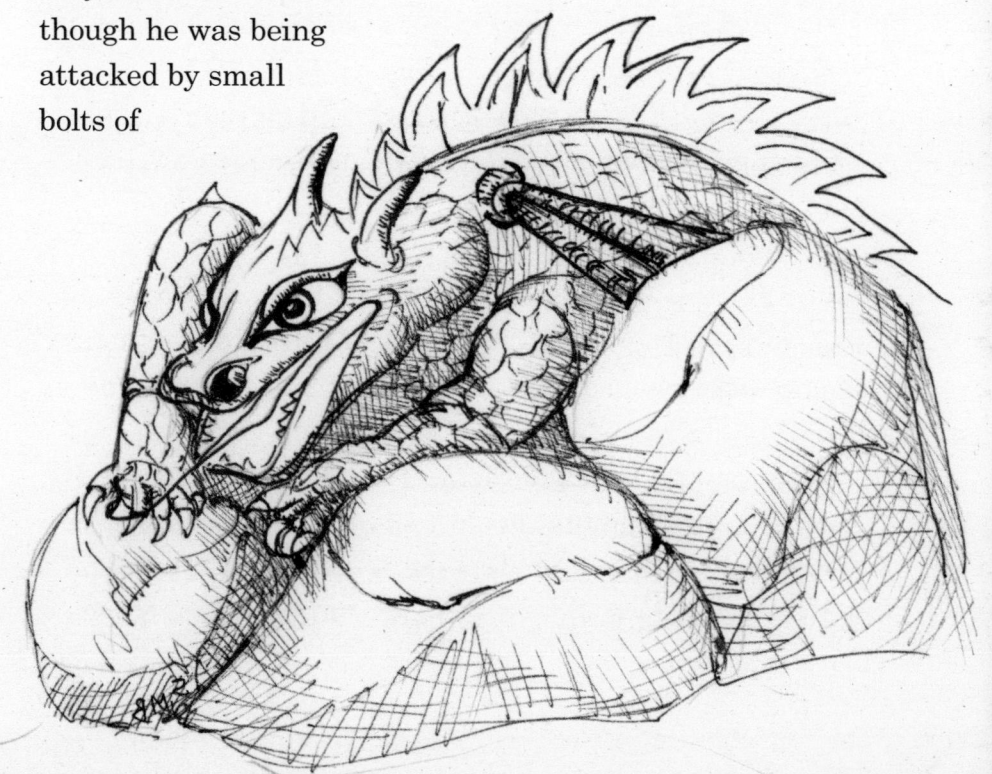

    Bluey saw that Uncle Chin's silver eyebrow dragons were darting all over his face, flashing red and blue fires; they made him look as though he was being attacked by small bolts of lightning. Aunty Lulu stood by his side not twitching a muscle. Agbad had an ugly frown on his face. Barry Basilisk's huge black eyes were bigger than ever, almost popping out of his head. His blue tongue darted between his black razor-sharp teeth and he was unfurling his enormous double wings and then snapping them shut again, making a booming noise like a cannon being fired.

Uncle Chin took a deep breath, and spoke. "Moma Draga, we all love you and desperately want to bring Smok home. But Dragu is a very powerful magician and his castle in the mountains of Transylvania is protected by an army of Snarks and bands of black dragons. Because of the special Basilisk spell that Smok used to protect himself, Dragu's attempt to destroy him has failed. We cannot attack Dragu directly, but we can trick him into taking some very special guests – some of us – into his throne room. If we can do that and let loose some especially strong spells, Barry can cast a spell to save Smok."

Bluey felt goosebumps run down his back and he jumped in fright. He saw that Uncle Chin was looking at him and Burney. So was everyone else. "Why? He was too frightened to even guess.

Uncle Chin turned back to Mama Draga. "Burney's mother, Auntie Burnice, has spider spies in Dragu's castle. Snip, Smok's dragon spider, managed to get away from Dragu by scuttling down a crack in the rocks. He met up with other spiders who are helping the resistance. They have reported that the stone Smok still stands tall in Dragu's throne room."

The spiders whistled and stomped their iron feet while Frizzy Lizzy hissed happily. Uncle Chin fixed his steely stare on Bluey and continued, "We are going to send a little group of our young dragons on a dangerous mission to rescue Smok. Our plan is that they will get themselves captured by Dragu. Yes, captured! We believe Dragu will take his prisoners to his throne room so he can gloat in front of Smok. But then, our most wonderful and powerful magic will begin"

Bluey's heart sank like stone. His tummy fire seemed to go out from black fear. "How," he wondered, "could a little dragon fight a monster like Dragu?" Poor Burney looked terrified. Moma Draga spurted jets of red flames and reared up in protest. Agbad jumped behind the boys and put his arms on their shoulders, as if to protect them. The spiders and Frizzy Lizzy went silent, holding their breath. Mrs P Hamster, seeing the terrified look on the boys' faces, waved her purple kerchief. Two humongous golden honey drops appeared in the air just in front of their noses. "Eat them," she commanded. Both dragons grabbed the magical honey drops, and chomped them down. Their tummy fires perked up, a warm glow spread through their bodies, and they relaxed a little.

Another humongous golden honey drop appeared right in front of Moma Draga's open mouth. She snaked out her tongue and ate it. It did the trick too. She stopped crying

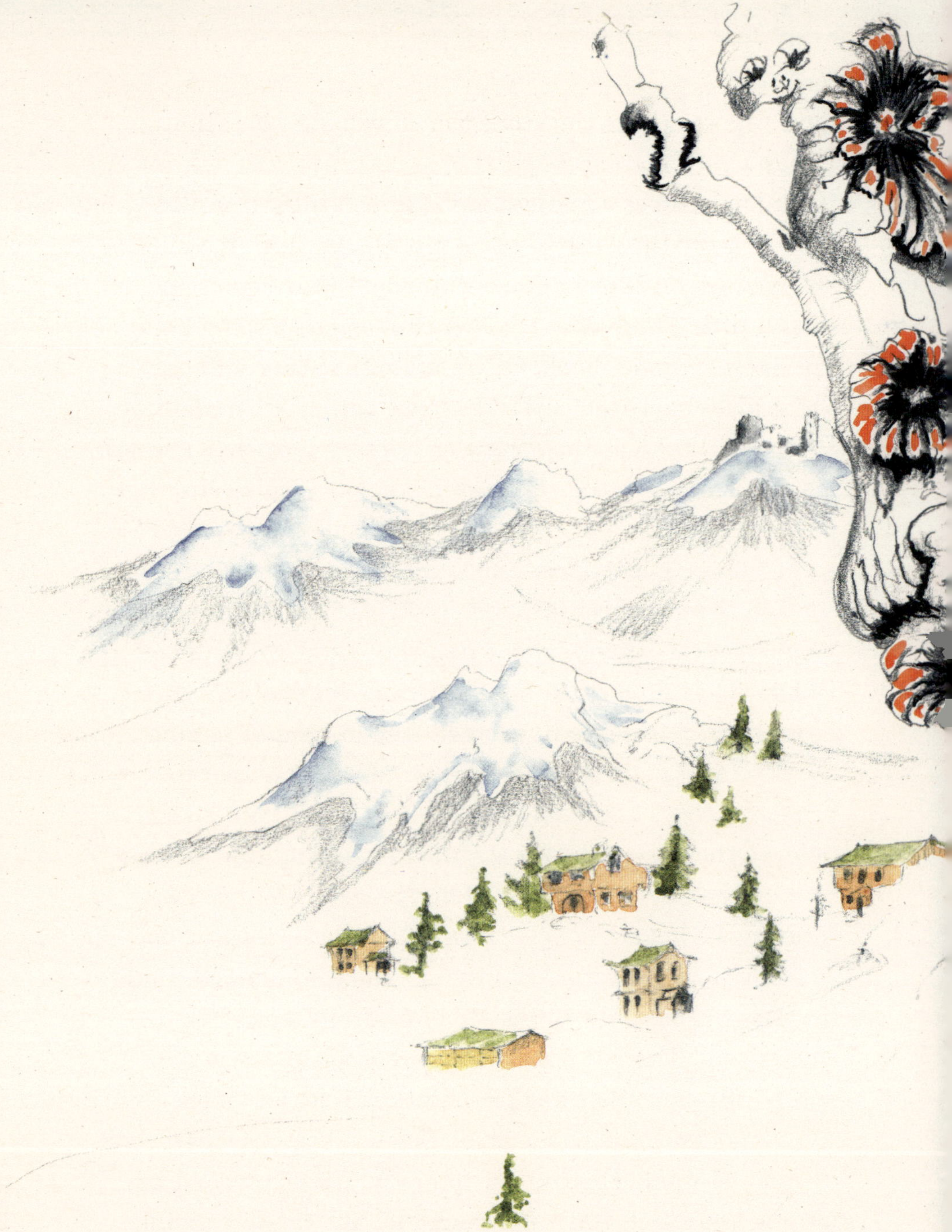

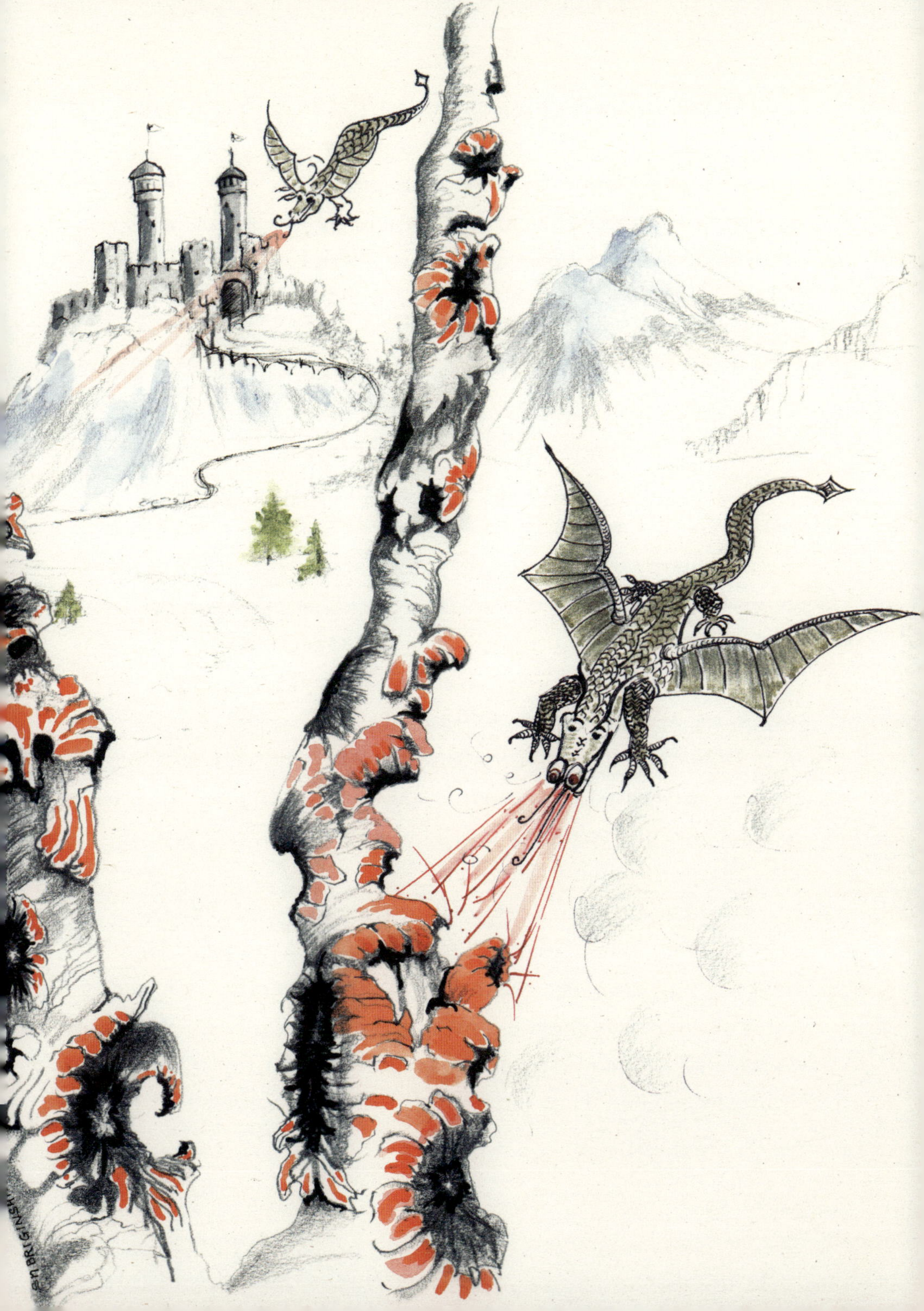

and relaxed in her rocking chair, letting out little puffs of white smoke through her nose. Her golden tears dried up as she thought about the dangerous plan. She knew about the powerful magic that Mrs P Hamster and Uncle Chin commanded. As for having Barry Basilisk there, "Well," she thought, "once upon a time he had ruled Transylvania from the very castle that Dragu now controls."

Agbad sat down with the boys, still holding them by the shoulders. They felt his strong hands, which made them feel less frightened.

Uncle Chin continued, "Agbad and Barry Basilisk will travel to Transylvania with you boys. I will also ask Melie Dragon to join you, and your special shapeshifting goblin friend, George, whose skills could be very helpful. Of course you will all take your own dragon spiders. Once you get into Dragu's throne room and our mighty magic starts, we will come to free Smok."

Bluey felt a rush of excitement. The spiders and Frizzy Lizzy whistled and stomped. But Burney had one big problem. "I don't have a dragon spider yet," he yelled out. "Does that mean I can't go?"

"Of course not," Mrs P Hamster answered. "You will go to the Fire Rocks dragons, and collect Jack spider. He must fly with you, and teach you to hunt Snarks. Both you boys and your friends have lots of training to do. And, we have lots of magic spells to prepare." Turning to Uncle Chin, she asked, "How long will it take to get everything ready, especially the extra special magic spells?"

Uncle Chin pointed a silver claw towards the window at the full yellow moon glimmering behind the scudding clouds and said, "It will be best to arrive when there is no moonlight. Barry has an old lair near Dragu's castle that he will take you to. Agbad's ruined village is nearby where the remnants of his people live in caves hidden from marauding Snarks and black dragons. They will surely help you. Your journey will start once the moon sets."

Bluey realized with a start that they had about four weeks to get ready. Gosh, he wondered, could we really do it?

Uncle Chin turned to Aunty Lulu, and said, "My love, as you are one of the most powerful shapeshifters in the world, I want you to spend time with George Goblin to work on tricks that might get the better of a magician like Dragu!"

Bluey saw Aunty Lulu's icy face turn from golden to warm pink as she blushed briefly. "Of course, I will help George," she said. Looking at Bluey she challenged him, "Just you wait and I will bring George to you disguised as a box of gooberberry pies!"

Uncle Chin turned to Mrs P Hamster: "Mrs P we have some very special spells to prepare. Where do you suggest we work on them?"

"At the Purple Possum, of course," Mrs P Hamster replied. "I will need Moma Draga to prepare travel food for the youngsters, and we will need to explore the bottom of my spell chest where I hide the very most powerful spells."

Moma Draga perked up at the mention of travel food. She offered to cook whatever was needed. Munch, who had jumped back onto her shoulder, was tapping in dragon code, "And, of course we will need some of those marvellous humongous honey drops to give courage to our young travellers."

That gave Mrs P Hamster a wonderfully wicked idea. Her green eyes glinted as she replied, "Why yes, of course, and maybe we will have some of those delicious treats to offer Dragu as well." Bluey thought that a very strange suggestion, but knew better than to interrupt.

"Now Agbad and Barry," Uncle Chin continued, "you two will be travelling to Transylvania with the young dragons and George Goblin, so it will be up to you to train them to be ready for the task."

Moma Draga brought the discussion to an end. It was near dawn, and they all needed to rest before starting their tasks.

Everyone obeyed her. The Chins conjured up their gleaming golden ball, stepped into it, and disappeared up the chimney. Mrs P Hamster waved her kerchief at the fireplace and disappeared in a cloud of purple smoke. Barry bid everyone goodbye, stomped to the door, unfurled his great double wings and flapped off into the glimmering dawn towards his lair by Dragon Rock. Agbad plucked a tired Frizzy Lizzy off the mantle shelf, and guided by Moma Draga, headed down the hallway to the spare bedroom.

Bluey and Burney still tingled from the humongous honey drops. Feeling both terrified and excited about the coming adventure, they headed up the hallway to their room. They threw themselves into their bunks as the first birdcalls of dawn sang out.

Moma Draga could not sleep. She was so excited, but also frightened, at what was being planned. She stoked up the fire and flopped back into her rocking chair to daydream about seeing her Smok again. She worried about the children being sent to Transylvania.

But, despite the drama of the night, she started to snore and fell asleep. The humongous honey drops had calmed her.

Only the dragon spiders on Septimus's web remained by the fading fire. They chatted away and ate more Snark pie, darting to and from the stone floor as they spotted crumbs of gooberberry slice that had been dropped. Excited that Jack was going to join them, they planned how best to help train Burney quickly in the art of Snark hunting. Old Munch was confident they could do it in time – after all, he had helped train Bluey and Septimus, who were an ace Snark hunting team.

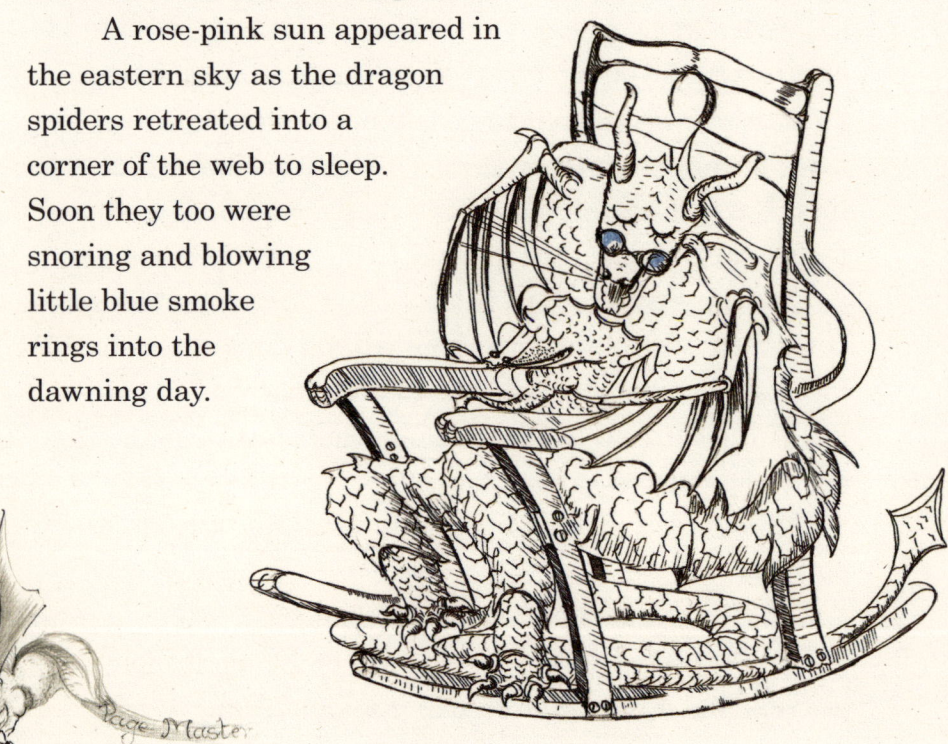

A rose-pink sun appeared in the eastern sky as the dragon spiders retreated into a corner of the web to sleep. Soon they too were snoring and blowing little blue smoke rings into the dawning day.

12
Getting ready

Bluey woke with a start. Burney was still asleep on his bunk. The morning chorus of birdcalls had long finished and golden sunlight streamed through the bedroom window. Everything was quiet. It was broken by the steely *clash* of scimitars being struck together, followed by another loud *clash*, then a high-pitched yodelling cry from Agbad.

Leaping out of bed, Bluey rushed down the hallway to see what was going on. Agbad was squatting in front of his magic circle below a red messenger star that was hovering, ready to fly out the window. Moma Draga was watching closely and smiling.

"What's going on?" demanded Bluey.

"Well, good morning, sleepyhead," Agbad replied. "I was just summoning your good friend Peter Pegasus to tell him our plans. I will ask Peter to fly me back to Transylvania while you and your friends ride with Barry Basilisk." Bluey's heart jumped with joy. The great Star Shepherd would be a strong fighter against Dragu.

Agbad continued, "After I talk with Peter, we will take Burney to the Red Fire Rocks dragons to fetch Jack. Also, we must ask Barry how he will fly you youngsters to Transylvania."

Bluey rushed off to wake Burney. Moma Draga prepared a late breakfast of fried blue duck eggs and toasted Snark slices, plus some strong elderberry tea to wake everyone properly. She also put out fresh gooberberry slices to snack on in case anyone was extra hungry.

Agbad stood up and tucked his glittering scimitars back into his heavy belt. One for each hand, thought Bluey. Agbad's black leather scabbard of Snark hunting javelins lay against the wall near Septimus's web. The three dragon spiders were scuttling about the kitchen, snatching crumbs. Old Munch led the search — after all, it was his kitchen too. Frizzy Lizzy sat on the table, licking at the honey pot with her darting blue tongue and catching insects that were silly enough to fly through the window.

Soon they all heard a loud *swish, swish* of strong wings outside and a clattering *clunk*, as Peter's bronze hooves landed on the stones outside Moma Draga's lair. He reared up, tapped with his bronze front hooves at

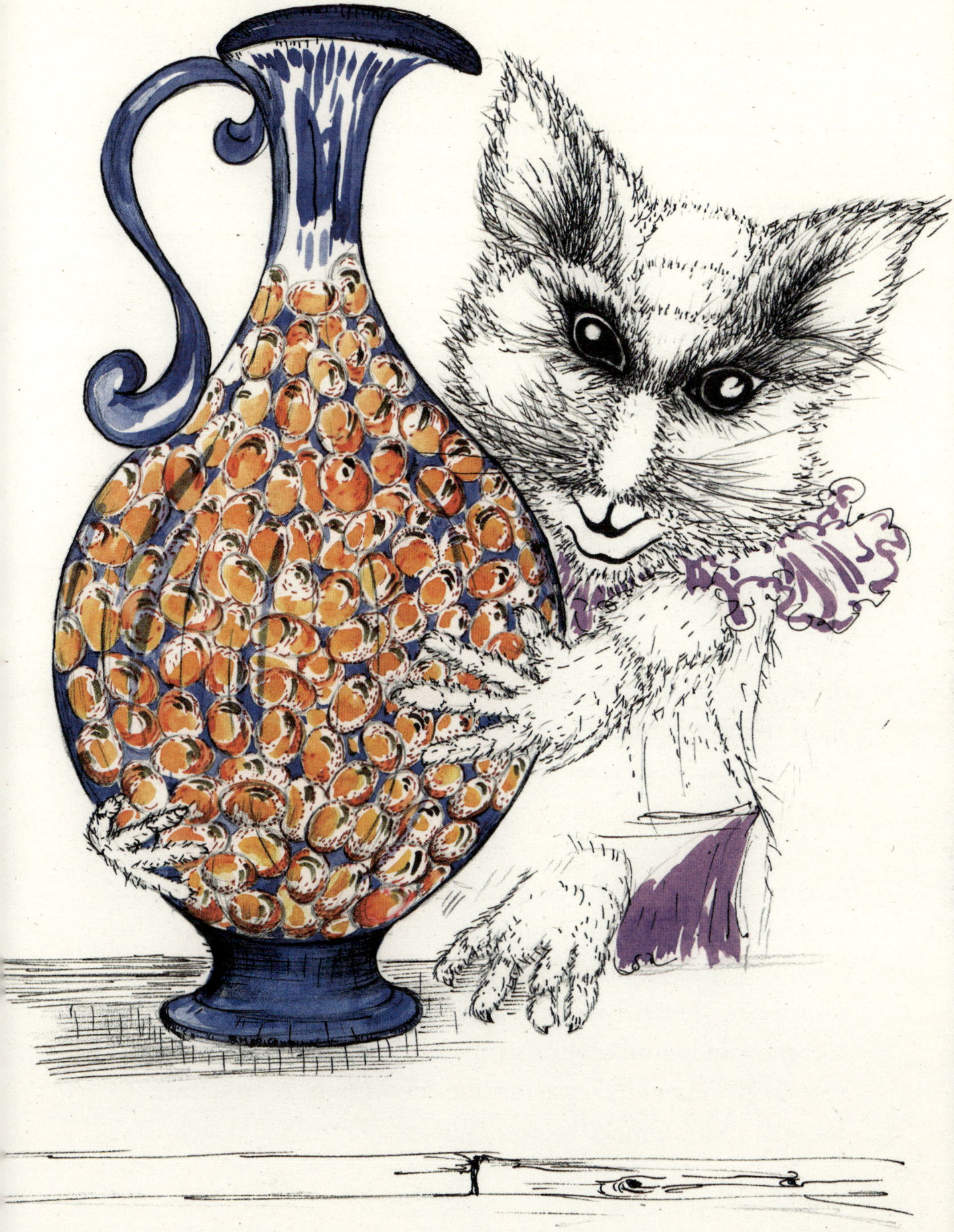

the door, and then trotted inside. Moma Draga greeted him with a big hug. Agbad yodelled a greeting. Peter gave a high-pitched whinny in reply. Everyone settled down so Agbad could explain to Peter their plan to rescue Smok.

Peter happily agreed to fly Agbad back to Transylvania. He was also willing to fight against Dragu and his minions. Agbad and Moma Draga were thrilled that the Star Shepherd would join the battle. His star magic and heavy bronze hooves would be deadly weapons against Snarks and black dragons. Peter then agreed to fly Agbad over to Dragon Rock to talk with Barry about how to transport the rescue team to Transylvania.

But first, Moma Draga wanted to go with Bluey and Burney to collect Jack dragon spider from the Red Rocks dragons. She and Bluey collected their dragon spiders and flapped off with Burney to the Red Rocks, leaving Agbad and Peter deep in conversation about how to fight Snarks and black dragons.

As the three dragons flew towards the old goblin forest, Moma Draga called the boys to dive down by the gnarled trees that marked the entrance to the forest. Landing, she explained that they needed to ask George's guardian, Mrs K Bracken, for her permission to let George join the rescue mission. Bluey showed them the way to the Bracken's tree stump home. Mrs K Bracken had not met Moma Draga, as she rarely travelled outside the goblin forest. Bluey only knew her as a kind old goblin with powerful shapeshifter skills.

Guiding Moma Draga and Burney into the middle of goblin village, he walked towards an ancient gnarled stump in front of a towering tree. Young goblins milled around to watch the big golden dragons. Bluey could see some older goblins peering at them through the tree branches – some were even watching, hanging upside down, just like bats.

As they neared the stump, Burney saw a large bunch of red roses sitting in a clay pot by the doorway. Bluey rushed over, grabbed the roses and threw them into the air. To Burney's amazement, the roses turned into a small black bat, which landed in front of the stump. The bat flickered into blue smoke and George appeared, laughing at his own trick. Then the stump cackled with laughter, grew arms, and a crinkly old face appeared with a hat of woven bracken on its head. It was Mrs K Bracken. She clapped her hands at George's antics, stood up, and bowed low to Moma Draga.

"I know why you are here, and I am so sorry to hear about your Smok," she said in a voice sounding like branches of trees creaking and squeaking in a high wind. "We had a visit from Uncle Chin and Aunty Lulu early this morning. They have a rescue plan, and want George to help. Aunty Lulu has started to share shapeshifter secrets with him. His first lesson was to turn himself into a bunch of red roses. But he failed – Bluey spotted the trick straight away."

Looking at Bluey, Mrs Bracken asked him how he knew that the roses were really George. He laughed, "Have you ever heard a bunch of roses giggling?"

"No," said Mrs K Bracken, "George clearly needs more training as giggling in his new disguise spoils the trick."

George looked disappointed, but Moma Draga reassured him that she had been tricked, and offered him a slice of gooberberry pie from her wicker basket. He grabbed it, thanked her, and sat down with Bluey and Burney to eat, while Moma Draga talked with Mrs K Bracken about the rescue mission.

Mrs K Bracken, settling down for a chat, pulled out an old clay pipe, stuffed it with some leaves, lighting it by flicking her fingers. A dense blue smoke swirled up, winding around the overhanging branch above her head. Bluey saw Munch and Septimus scuttle up the tree and start to snort in the smoke. Soon the dragon spiders were hissing and giggling as they staggered on the branches. One by one they tipped over and fell to the ground, laying on their backs like dead beetles, except they were both blowing little blue smoke rings.

Mrs K Bracken laughed, apologised, and explained to Moma Draga that she had used giggle leaf in her pipe, as it was more relaxing than regular leaf. She reassured Moma Draga that the two spiders would be all right, except for some ringing in their ears and pains in their heads for the rest of the day.

Moma Draga was not happy about that, but she was glad that Mrs K Bracken had agreed that George could join the rescue mission.

Next,
Moma Draga
wanted to take the
boys to the Red Rocks lair. They said their goodbyes.
George promised to practise hard with Aunty Lulu on
his shapeshifting. Bluey challenged him to look like
Frizzy Lizzy or Whisky Dog the next time they met.
George accepted the challenge in exchange for more
gooberberry slices.

The three dragons, with their two very sorry dragon spiders, flew off towards the Red Rocks lair. But they didn't notice the strange looking knobbly stick hanging from the bottom of Munch's flying harness.

Swooping east as they left the Blue Tier, the dragons flew down the long green valley towards the sparkling blue sea. As they neared the coast, Bluey could see the great pile of rocks called the Gardens, where Melie dragon and her flying Whisky Dog lived with old Meff dragon. He longed to drop-in and see them and hear the yodelling of Melie's dragon spider, Sam. However, collecting Jack was today's mission. They turned south and headed towards the green Garden pastures and the Red Rocks lair.

As they approached the lair, a single golden dragon, Burnbox (Fireguts's brother), flapped up to greet them. He called out, and pointed to Jack, who was riding on his shoulder. Abruptly, Burnbox wheeled in the sky and dived down towards to a clump of old trees near the beach. A Snark was running for cover, but not quickly enough.

Burnbox swerved, and dropped straight down over the Snark's back. Jack jumped off and sank his fangs into the Snark's back, and then quickly looped a link of chain mail web over his snout. The Snark reared up and twisted its head to bite at Jack, but the chain mail held its snout closed. Jack's venom started to work and the Snark fell over, howling and gnashing its teeth in frustration. Jack jumped off, and ran in to push the Snark's tickle button on its tummy. As he did so, the Snark laughed hideously, then it stopped breathing and fell silent.

Landing nearby, Moma Draga hooted in joy at the quick end to the Snark. Bluey and Burney yelled in support. Despite the pain in their heads, Munch and Septimus hooted and stomped. Then, seemingly out of nowhere, George appeared.

"How did you do that?" a surprised Bluey asked. George grinned and disappeared. This time, Munch spotted the piece of knobby wood attached to the bottom of his flying harness. Moma laughed and clapped her claws at George's trick, and said, "You've shown us why we need a shapeshifter on the rescue mission."

Jack danced and glowed with pride at his demonstration of tickling a Snark to death. Burnbox rewarded him with a huge piece of gooberberry pie.

Moma Draga introduced Burney to Burnbox and Jack. Burnbox explained that Fireguts could not be here to greet Burney, as he was still recovering from his terrible wing wound. He promised that Burney would receive excellent Snark hunting training from Jack, so that they would become an expert Snark hunting team, like Bluey and Septimus.

Burnbox went into the lair and came out with a package wrapped in polished grey Snark skin. He unwrapped it and bowed as he gave Burney the shiny leather flying harness and flying goggles that Fireguts once used. Jack scuttled over to Burney, climbed up to his shoulder, and helped hang the flying harness from his ear.

Moma Draga and Burney thanked Burnbox and, surprising the boys, she told them that they would now visit old Meff dragon. There was urgency in her voice as she told Burnbox, "We must keep going. Every day we have things to get ready for Smok's rescue mission, before the moon sets." Spreading her wings, she leapt up and flapped into the sky, heading north along the coast to Meff's lair at the Garden rocks.

Working fast, Bluey and Septimus made sure that Burney had put on the flying harness correctly so Jack could jump into it. George turned himself into a monkey, and jumped onto Bluey's back as the boys leapt into the air and flapped fast to catch up with Moma Draga. She was letting out red jets of flame and smoke with each flap of her big wings. Smaller and more agile, it didn't take long for the boys to catch her, and they flew in formation; Moma Draga in the lead followed by Bluey and Burney, looking like large golden ducks that glowed in the bright midday sun.

The jumble of Red Rocks at the Gardens was soon below them, and they circled, ready to land on the rock ledge by the entrance to Meff's lair. A small furry creature hurtled up into the air to greet them. It was Whisky Dog, flapping his wings madly to keep pace with the dragons. He yelped a greeting and plummeted back to the ground where he bounced around in excitement, trying to lick the dragon's faces as they landed. Melie rushed out to see what the commotion was about. Seeing them, Sam spider yodelled a Snark hunting song in greeting. Old Meff dragon wasn't there to greet them. Moma Draga was disappointed and asked Melie where Meff had gone. Melie told her that

Agbad, a fierce fighting dwarf, had visited earlier in the morning, flying in on Peter Pegasus, of all creatures. Then after a quick chat, they had flown off with Meff to see Barry Basilisk.

"Did Agbad explain our mission to rescue Smok?" Moma Draga asked.

"Oh, yes," Melie replied. "Meff gave permission for Sam and I to join the boys on the mission."

Moma Draga sighed with relief. The boys beamed with delight on hearing that Melie would be joining them. Moma Draga commanded, "Then, we must all fly to Barry's lair by Dragon Rock at Skeleton Point. We have a problem to solve."

She leapt in to the air and headed south, down the coast, back towards the Red Rocks and Skeleton Point. The young dragons followed, but were starting to tire as Skeleton Point came into view. Moma Draga swooped down and landed next to Dragon Rock.

They could see the huge shape of Barry sitting on his favourite rock by the entrance to his lair. Peter Pegasus, Agbad and old Meff were with him in deep conversation as Moma Draga and the young dragons approached. She greeted them, and asked, "How are your plans going to get the rescue team to Transylvania?"

Barry turned, saying in his deep thunderous voice, "Not well! Peter will fly Agbad over to Transylvania, but taking three young dragons, a goblin and a flying dog is just too many for me to carry on my back. We need a large wicker basket, bigger than the one you carry, for them all to fit into. We don't know anyone who has such a thing!"

Everyone looked very worried but Munch had a plan. He started to tap urgently on Moma Draga's ear. "Oh my, what a wonderful idea!" she exclaimed, her golden eyes gleaming in pleasure. "How about a big basket woven out of chain mail spider web?

"It would be perfect if it could be made in time," Barry replied.

Munch scuttled over to Septimus and Jack. Furious hissing and hooting came from the dragon spiders for a few minutes. Then Munch scuttled back up to Moma Draga's ear and tapped again. As she listened her eyes got wider and wider. Munch's taps stopped, and Moma Draga reached into her travel basket and whipped out three big slices of gooberberry pie, one for each spider. She then told everyone about Munch's plan.

"All the dragon spider families in the Blue Tier, the Gardens, Red Rocks and here on Skeleton Point have expert weavers. Munch will ask them all to gather at the Purple Possum where they can weave the travelling basket. Naturally they must be rewarded. So my job will be to bake enough Snark pies to keep them happy while they weave fast to get the basket finished before the moon sets." They all thought that this was a perfect solution.

The young dragons were very tired from the day's excitement, so Moma Draga decided it was time to return home to the Blue Tier for dinner. She reminded them that tomorrow Burney's Snark hunting training would start in earnest, and Aunty Lulu would come again to the goblin forest to work with George on shapeshifting tricks. Moma Draga would also need to have an early start to be at the Purple Possum to bake piles of Snark pies, to keep the basket-weaving spiders happy. It was going to be a very busy time for everybody.

The dragons flapped into the red setting sun and headed homewards; Peter Pegasus flying beside them with Agbad sitting proudly on his back.

13 Spells and potions

Next morning, Moma Draga got everyone out of bed at dawn. She cooked a quick breakfast and flew off to the Purple Possum before the boys had finished eating. Before rushing off, Moma told Bluey to take special care of Burney, and most importantly, told Burney to carefully follow Septimus and Jack's Snark-hunting training instructions

Agbad and Peter Pegasus planned their return to Barry's lair to prepare for the trip to Transylvania. They were sending Mail Orbs to and from Burnice (Burney's mom) for Snip who was living at Burnice's lair. Brave

Snip, was leading the gang of spiders which were creeping into Dragu's castle to spy on him.

After breakfast, Bluey spent time showing Burney how to wear his flying goggles. Burney was thrilled how the goggles glowed blue, and went *zip-zip-zip* as they let him see through clumps of tree branches or bushes on the ground. Jack, by tapping and tugging on Burney's ear, showed him how he could direct Burney to swoop and turn as they hunted a Snark. They passed the morning with many practice runs, hunting pretend Snarks. It was nearly time for lunch, when Bluey spotted a Snark just near the entrance to the goblin forest. Nearby, he was shocked to see Mrs K Bracken enjoying the sun, sitting in her favourite spot, smoking her pipe full of giggle leaf.

Calling to Burney, Bluey pointed at the Snark who, having spotted Mrs K Bracken, was galloping fast towards her. Both dragons dived at once towards the Snark. Bluey tried to get ahead of the Snark. Burney flew over its back to give Jack a chance to jump.

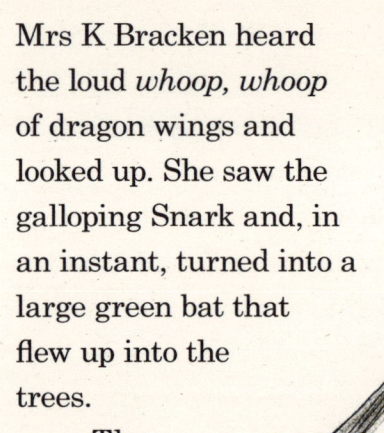

Mrs K Bracken heard the loud *whoop, whoop* of dragon wings and looked up. She saw the galloping Snark and, in an instant, turned into a large green bat that flew up into the trees.

The Snark swerved to give chase to another terrified goblin running for his life towards his tree house. Burney could now see everything clearly through his goggles. He swooped in over the Snark's back, letting Jack jump off. Septimus joined him, having leapt off Bluey's back at the same time. Septimus sank his fangs into the Snark's back while Jack looped chain mail web over its snout. It roared, howled and fell thrashing to its side. Jack rushed in and pushed its pink tickle button. The Snark stopped thrashing, howled horribly with evil laughter and fell silent.

Bluey and Burney were ecstatic. They congratulated their spiders, rewarding them with big pieces of gooberberry pie. Mrs K Bracken flapped down, flicking from a green bat to her normal wizened shape, and thanked them all for such quick action. Then, looking very serious, she reached into her brown leather pouch, pulling out a strange looking package made of woven bracken fronds. Inside it was a collection of small wooden shapes. She rummaged around and suddenly exclaimed, "Ah, ha, I have found them!" She held aloft three small dragons carved from white bone. They were painted in golden hues and had shimmering green runes running around their bodies.

"Here is one for each of you brave dragons, plus an extra one for Melie. Wear them around your necks when you arrive in Transylvania. They are powerful magic Tree Guards. They will make your scales look just like any tree or shrub you are standing near. George does not need one, as he is a true shapeshifter. Use them well on your mission to rescue Papa Smok."

Bluey and Burney bowed low as they thanked Mrs K Bracken for her gifts. Jack and Septimus hooted, clapping in appreciation. With a muffled squawk Ping-Ling landed to pick up the dead Snark. Bluey saw that Ping-Ling was carrying in his beak a glowing purple Message Orb with the words writhing around its middle:

Purple Possum

They all knew this must have come from Mrs P Hamster.

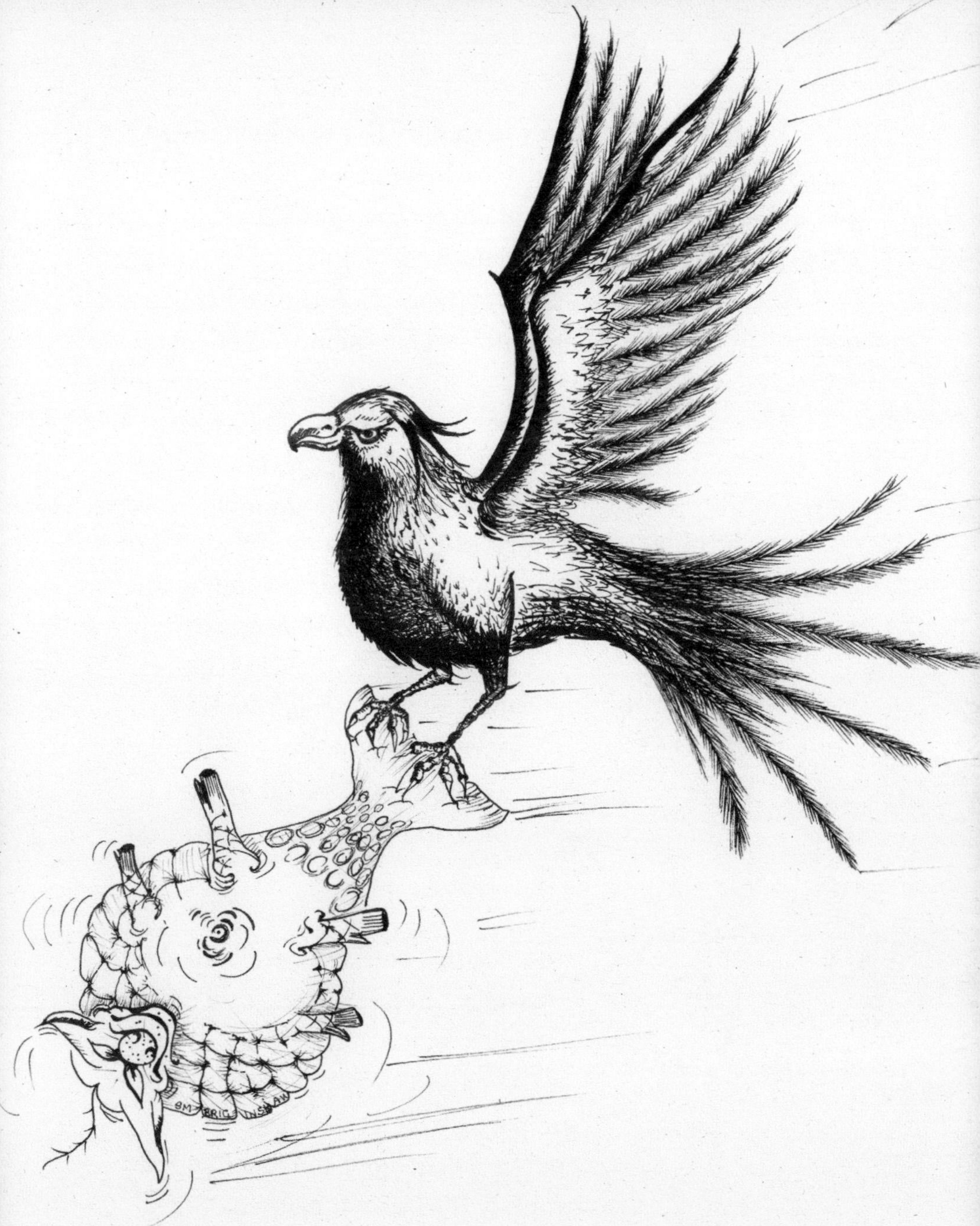

Ping-Ling dropped the Orb at Bluey's feet. Bluey reached down and opened it. Inside was a piece of parchment with fiery purple lettering that flared and glowed if it was alive. He read it out loud:

Fly immediately to the Purple Possum.
Mighty magic is being brewed.
Uncle Chin is waiting!"

Before Bluey could move, the parchment dissolved in a puff of purple smoke. Ping-Ling grabbed the dead Snark in his beak and the now empty Messenger Orb in a claw and leapt into the air. The boys said goodbye to Mrs K Bracken, flew into the air and headed off, up and over the high hills towards the Purple Possum.

As they approached to land they could see lots of activity. Purple sparks and swirls of silver black smoke were flying out the living room chimney. White smoke filled with red and green sparks belched out of the kitchen chimney. The green grass at the back was covered in black dragon spiders who were weaving coils of chain mail web as they munched on Snark pies. Other spiders were weaving the new web into shimmering silver ropes. Still more spiders were taking the ropes and joining them together into an enormous flying basket that was already taking shape.

On a long trestle table outside the kitchen door they saw piles of newly baked Snark pies, ready for chomping. Much to their delight there was even a pile of gooberberry slices at one end of the table. They rushed inside to find a crowded living room.

There was Meff dragon, Melie and Whisky Dog who, of course, bounced at the boys and greeted them by slurping their noses. George stood nearby chatting with Aunty Lulu. Barry Basilisk was standing with Agbad and Peter Pegasus near a huge wooden chest. It was bound with silver iron chains and topped with a large rock that seemed to be watching over the room. Mrs P Hamster and Uncle Chin were in heated discussion nearby.

Seeing the boys, Uncle Chin beckoned them over. But before they moved a step closer, Moma Draga popped her head around the door to announce that a fresh batch of gooberberry slices plus minced Snark pies were ready to be chomped. With shouts of delight everyone, except Peter Pegasus and Mrs P Hamster, headed for the kitchen.

Bluey and Burney tried to join the others, but their feet seemed stuck to the floor. Mrs P Hamster waved her purple kerchief at them and pointed her paw towards the magic chest. Their feet came unstuck and they found themselves moving towards the shaking and jiggling chest. Peter put a huge bronze hoof on the rock to hold the lid of the chest tight shut. Mrs P Hamster waved her kerchief again and produced a large silver key, seemingly from thin air. While Peter held the lid shut, she unlocked all the padlocks that held the chains.

They fell off with loud jangling *clunks* to the wooden floor. Motioning Peter to stand aside, she waved her purple kerchief and the rock vanished. The chest was totally still, but Bluey could feel that the air around it was humming and vibrating with powerful magic.

Mrs P Hamster gently opened the carved lid of the chest. A flock of purple stars flew up and danced in a circle around the room. Peter took a deep breath and huffed what looked like a deep blue fog at them. The stars stopped dancing and huddled together over Peter's head. Bluey remembered why Peter was called the Star Shepherd – he could make stars obey him. Mrs P Hamster leaned into the chest muttering something. Perhaps a spell Bluey thought. As he watched, she lifted out a bulging leather pouch. Runes of golden fire ran over it, flickering and flashing. She tugged at a dragon symbol attached to a sliver cord, which held the neck of the pouch closed.

Uncle Chin appeared by Mrs P Hamster's side. Taking the pouch, and holding the golden dragon symbol in his claws, he muttered an opening spell. The symbol woke up and slithered down to the floor pulling the silver cord with it. The mouth of the pouch dropped open and a jumble of small purple stone amulets fell into his outstretched claw.

Each one was set with silver and gold runes. Mrs P Hamster lifted one up and explained that each member of Smok's rescue team would be given an amethyst amulet to help protect them from Dragu's powerful magic. Bluey wondered how they worked, because for all the world, they looked just like the purple potato chips that Moma Draga often cooked.

Mrs P Hamster seemed to read his mind as she suddenly whirled an amulet around her head and uttered a high-pitched shrieking spell, causing everyone to cover their ears. A fierce Orb of purple fire appeared around the amulet as it whirled round and round her head. The purple Orb flickered out, but now the amulet itself glittered with purple fires that flared and pulsed, and then snapped out. She handed the amulet to Uncle Chin who held it tight in his claw and muttered a strange Chinese spell. Opening his claw, Bluey could see that the amulet was now attached to a shiny golden chain with a dragon clasp. Uncle Chin handed the amulet back to Mrs P Hamster who gently put the chain around Bluey's neck, snapping the clasp shut.

To his amazement, Bluey's fears disappeared. He even felt eager to start the rescue mission. He thanked Mrs P Hamster and showed her the Tree Guard that Mrs K Bracken had given them. "Wear it well," she said, as she waived her purple kerchief at the Tree Guard, which flew out of Bluey's hand and attached itself to the golden chain around his neck.

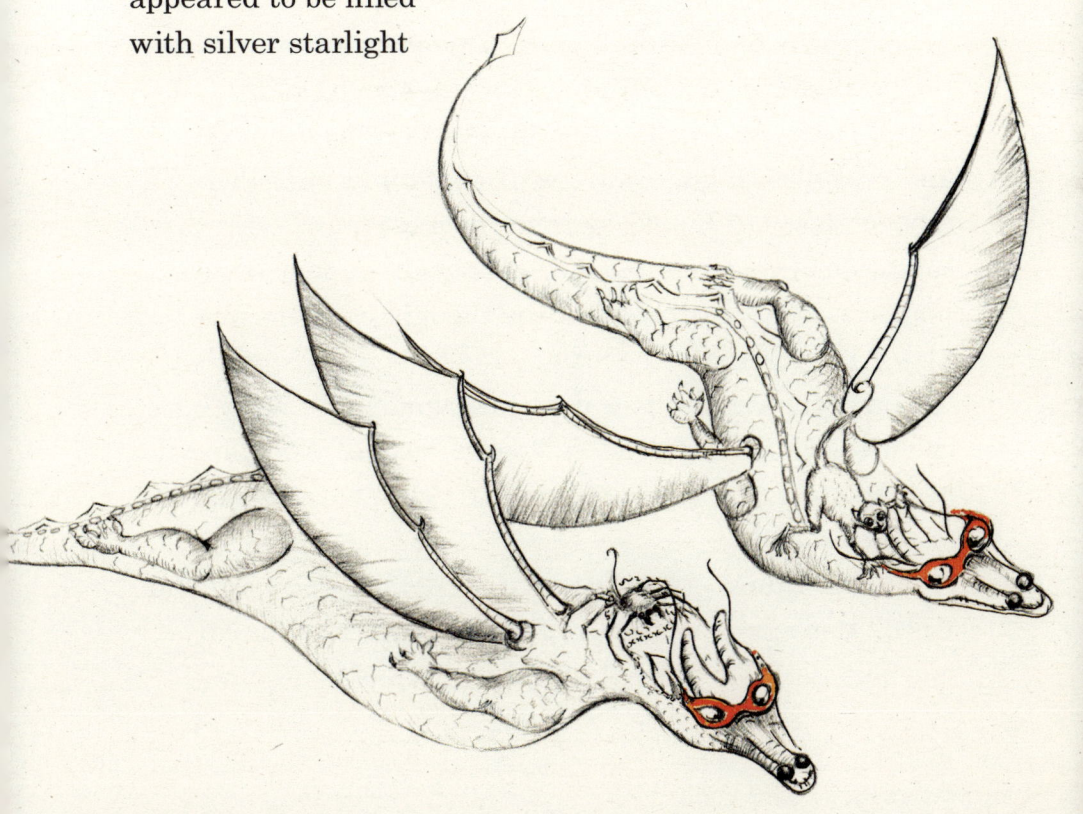

Mrs P Hamster called over all members of the rescue team and gave each an amulet. When Burney's turn came, his amulet pulsed with red fires. Melie and Whisky Dog each received an amulet that pulsed with silver fires; Agbad's pulsed with green fires, Peter's appeared to be filled with silver starlight while Barry's glowed orange like burning coal. Then came George's turn.

Bluey wondered, how could a shapeshifter wear an amulet?

Mrs P Hamster and Uncle Chin fixed that problem. They give him one that would become invisible when he changed shape. They did this, after much magical incantation that produced an amulet, which flickered with purple fires when George stood still, but faded when he moved, then vanished when he changed shape. George was grateful, because until this amulet sat snugly around his neck, he had been terrified of being captured by Dragu.

"Now we must deal with some very special magic that Uncle Chin and I have made," declared Mrs P Hamster. She reached into the still jiggling chest and pulled out a huge shimmering, glimmering, silver-topped glass jar. Inside, swirled the most marvellous collection of golden humongous honey drops that Bluey had ever seen. He drooled at the thought of eating one. Mrs P Hamster saw the look on his face and whipped off the lid of the jar. A honey drop flew up and hit Bluey on the nose. Then it hovered in front of his face, and danced around, as if challenging him to snatch it from the air and chomp it down.

"No, Bluey," Mrs P Hamster commanded in a loud voice, "don't try to catch it. These are for Dragu. No one else is to eat them. I will give each of you young dragons a small jar of these dangerous honey drops to carry. If Dragu captures you, I am sure he will take them to eat himself. Then you will see what they do!" Bluey's face dropped in disappointment. "Don't worry Bluey," Mrs P Hamster said, "once your Papa Smok is rescued you can have as many yummy golden humongous honey drops as you can eat."

    Now it was Uncle Chin's turn to reach into the still heaving chest. He pulled out three small travelling boxes of Chinese checkers, each tied neatly with silver ribbon. Bluey noticed that the chest had stopped heaving and jiggling. How strange, Bluey thought, because the checker boxes looked very ordinary. But when Uncle Chin pulled the ribbon off one of the boxes, Bluey saw they were far from ordinary. The lid flew open with a loud snap. All the checkers shot out, letting off red sparks, whistling as they flew around the room like a pack of angry fireflies. Together, they swirled out the door into the hallway and hovered by the long mirror on the wall. Each checker flashed red fire that flickered out before landing on the glass. With a *click, click, click* they all stuck to the mirror.

Uncle Chin and Mrs P Hamster looked very pleased with their demonstration of the dance of the checkers. Bluey asked, "Uncle Chin, how do we play with them?"

"You don't," he replied. "Just make sure that if Dragu captures you and takes you into his throne room that at least one box of checkers is opened and dropped on the floor." Turning to George, he said, "That is one of your tasks, if your friends can't do it. We know that Dragu likes playing with magic checkers, so we hope he will look in one of these boxes."

They were interrupted by Moma Draga bursting into the room with a big tray of freshly baked gooberberry slices and more minced Snark pies. "Eat up and enjoy," she ordered.

As she put down the steaming tray she wailed loudly, "My Smok is waiting to be rescued. Finish your preparations and hurry off to Transylvania." She burst into great golden tears as she rushed back to the kitchen. Bluey ran to comfort her, but Mrs P Hamster held him back, telling him to join the others as there was still lots of planning to do.

Everyone then grabbed something to eat and sat down to listen to Barry and Agbad tell them what to expect when they arrived in Transylvania.

14
Transylvania – Dragutransylvania

The next few days disappeared in a whirl of activity. There were Snark hunting lessons for Burney and planning meetings at the Purple Possum, plus they had to collect their travel gear. Most difficult for dragons used to flying everywhere were trips to the mountains with Agbad and Barry to practise cliff climbing – this was particularly important. Dragu's castle sat high on a steep cliff. It had to be climbed on foot so they that they could approach the entrance gate as close as possible without being seen by Dragu's black dragon guards.

Finally, late one evening, a message came from the team of spider weavers to say that the flying basket was ready. On hearing this Moma Draga hooted with joy. Now the rescue team could make their last preparations

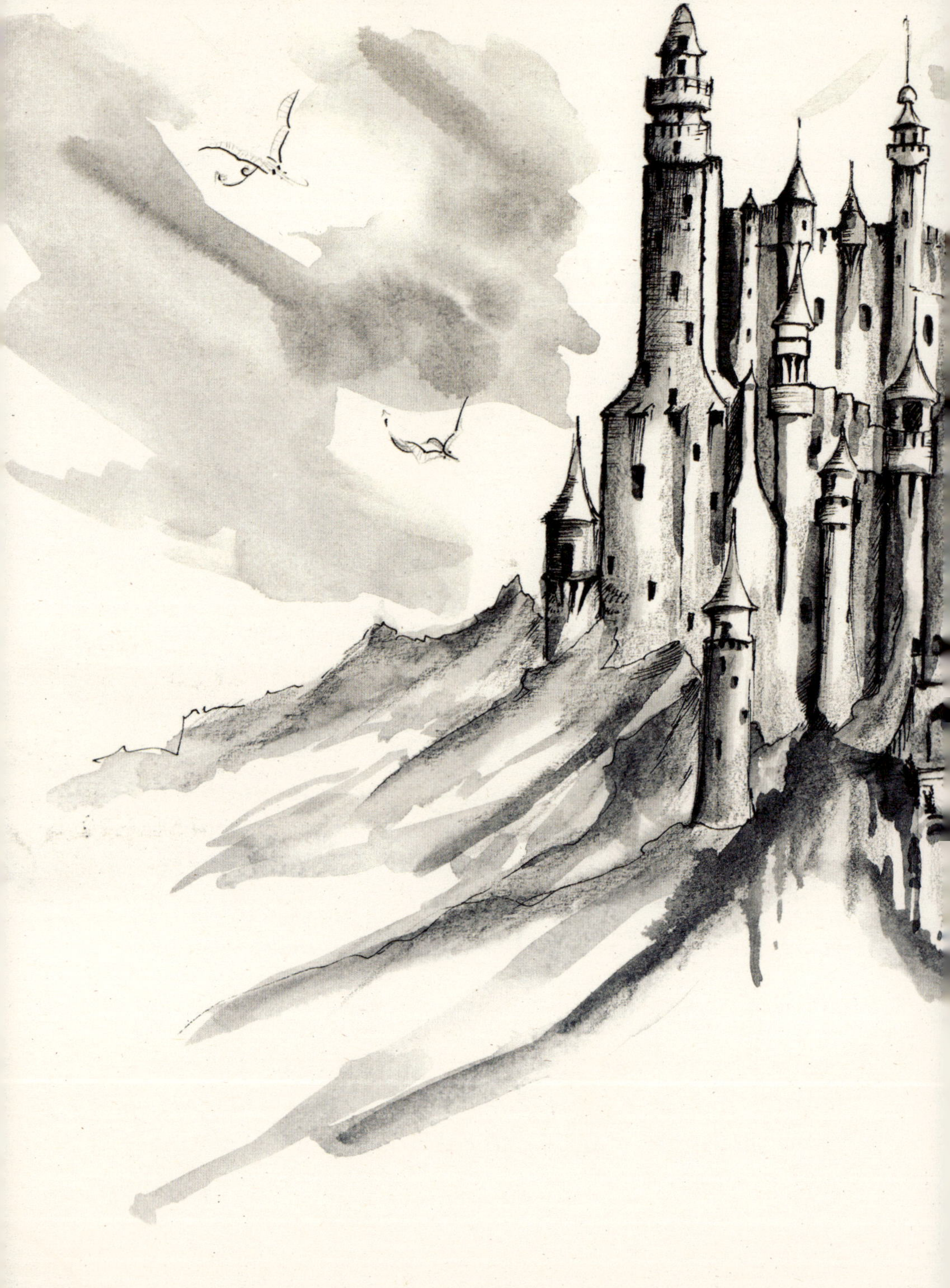

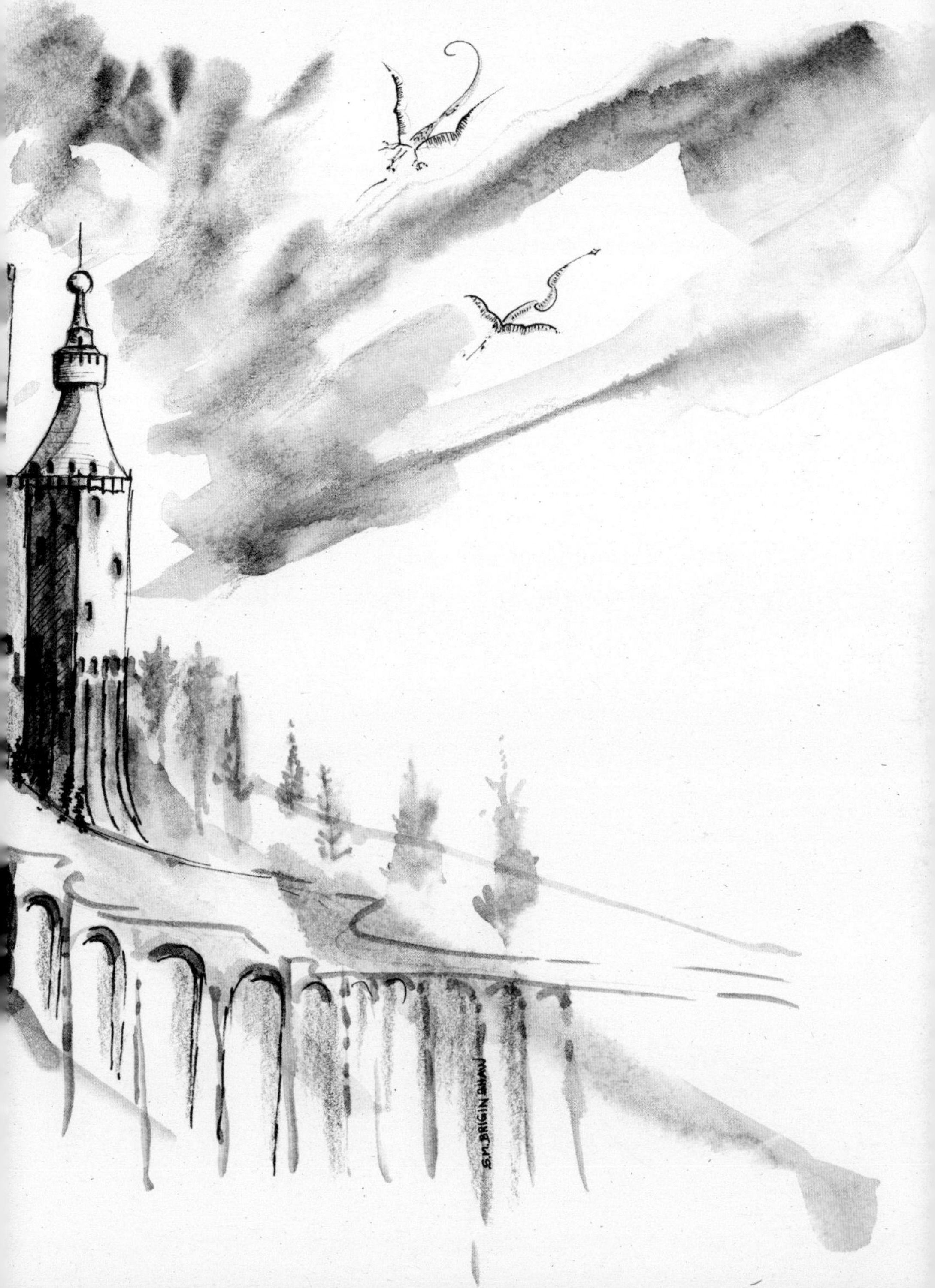
S.M.BRIGIN SHAW

to leave for Transylvania. Straight after breakfast the next morning everyone rushed off to the Purple Possum to test the basket. Barry and Agbad had to be sure that the rescue team could fit in the basket with all their travelling supplies. As they landed, Moma Draga was waiting with a basket of extra gooberberry slices and Snark pies.

There stood the big travel basket, woven from chain mail spider web, shimmering silver in the morning rays of sunshine. While it looked fragile, as spider webs always do, they all knew that it was as strong as could be.

"All right," Barry yelled in his loud deep voice. "Rescue team, climb in! Bluey and Burney, you stand here on this side. George and Melie, you stand on the other side. Place your travel bags and extra gear in the middle, and sit Whisky Dog on top."

They did as they were told, and Bluey even managed to add Moma Draga's small wicker basket of baked goodies. Then, just as they were wondering when they should get out, Barry unfurled his huge double wings. He leapt into the air and grabbed the flying ropes. Tugging them taut, he flapped hard and with a sharp jerk the basket lifted into the air. They all gasped in shock.

Mrs P Hamster waved her purple kerchief and Uncle Chin fired off a flight of powerful firecrackers that flashed and dazzled in the morning sun. Agbad, sitting astride Peter Pegasus, swooped in to join them and yelled, "Hold on tight, off we go to Transylvania!"

They all looked at one another, too shocked to shout goodbye, their claws tightly grabbing the edge of the basket. To stop himself falling off, Whisky Dog dug his claws into the travel packs. Up, up, into the bright midday sky flew Barry with the basket, closely followed by Peter.

On the horizon they could see a band of big black clouds. Barry headed swiftly towards them. Soon damp, grey mists flew past the basket of anxious faces, as the ground vanished from sight beneath them. The clouds got blacker and they started to see blue and red lightning bolts followed by great peals of thunder. Peter's wings made their *whoop-whooping* noise nearby, but he was now out of sight. Barry flew closer and closer to the black thunderheads.

Next thing they saw was a great bolt of blue lightning striking Barry's back. It sparked and flickered, running around his double wings, causing them to look like flapping pools of electric blue water. Then another great clap of thunder boomed around them. The travel basket jerked and they felt it start moving at tremendous speed. Whisky Dog crouched down and dug his claws even deeper into the travel packs. Wind whistled and howled around their ears.

Suddenly, the howling wind stopped and the basket seemed to be drifting. Above them they could still hear Barry's wings beating as the basket flew over a strange black landscape. There were no clouds. Starlight glinted off craggy cliffs and red lights glimmered from windows in the high towers of a grand castle that sat atop one of the cliffs. Peter flew by their side, as he and Barry silently glided down into a nearby black chasm.

Taking care how he landed the travel basket, Barry let go the flying ropes and announced in a hushed voice, "Welcome my brave team you have arrived in Transylvania! Now, come quickly, into my lair."

Everyone grabbed their travel bags in shocked silence. Even Whisky Dog did not make a sound. Barry struck a flint that sparked a small red lamp and hurried towards a gap in the rocks. Anxiously following, they squeezed through to find themselves in front of a shiny black slab of rock set into the cliff. The slab was fire-scarred and battered, as if something had tried to push it aside – as indeed the black dragons and Snarks had tried many times.

Barry tapped on the rock and muttered a spell. He then grabbed some rocks that stuck out beneath the slab and pushed upwards. The rock creaked a bit then silently slid up into the overhanging cliff. Barry gave the red lamp to Agbad and motioned them all inside.

The team scurried down a long dark hallway and around a corner, which opened into a large room lit up by yellow and green glowworm lights, just like their lairs at home. Without stopping, Barry turned around and headed back up the hallway. He brought in the travel basket, and with a muffled thud, he closed the rock door. Returning to the big room, he lit the fire, and asked them to sit down.

The young dragons were so shocked by the speed of events that they just sat there. Only George, who was used to dark places in the old goblin forest, seemed at home. Agbad started by explaining that, in case Dragu had spies on the Blue Tier or at the Purple Possum, Mrs P Hamster and Uncle Chin had planned that the team would leave without any announcement. Even Moma Draga had agreed, since the idea was to help keep everyone safe.

A thunderstorm had loomed on the horizon, so it was an ideal time to fly. Both Barry and Peter used the power of lightning to jump great distances from one place to another. This, Barry explained, was why he and Peter had flown into the blue lightning bolt. Barry grinned. "You dragons have never flown like that," he said.

Agbad pulled off his big hat. Out jumped Frizzy Lizzy and Snap, who scuttled over to join Septimus, Jack, and Sam by the fire. But Frizzy decided to run up the rock wall to perch on top of the mantelpiece. As she jumped onto the top of the mantelpiece she froze and let out a sharp *hiss*. Barry lent over to see what was wrong. There lay Snip, Papa Smok's dragon spider. He had fire scars on his back, and one leg was bandaged in healing moss. But most importantly, he was alive!

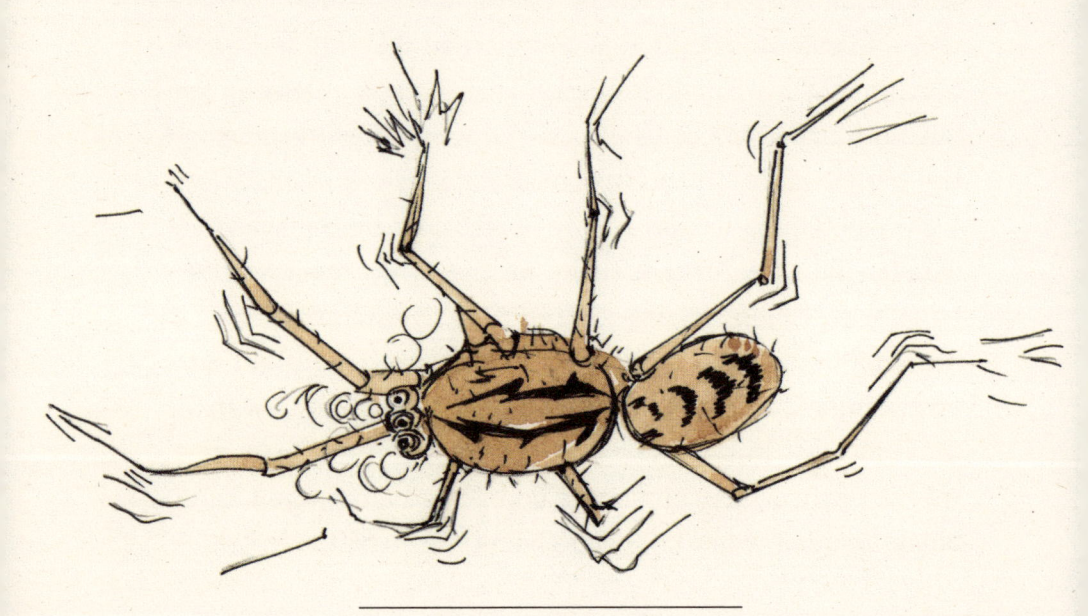

Barry picked up Snip and cradled him in his huge claw, and then put him down by the warm fire with the other dragon spiders. They gathered around Snip to hear him quietly hiss out his story, which Snap translated into dragon code so Agbad could tell the rest of the team.

Yesterday Snip had been spying on Dragu in the throne room when one of the black dragons spotted him on the wall. Fortunately, instead of alerting Dragu who was hurling fire bolts at stone Smok, the dragon had tried to catch Snip. But Snip had managed to slip into a crack in the wall, just as the dragon spat a blast of red fire at him. The dragon fire had scorched his back and burnt one leg. Snip had scuttled out of the castle and then painfully crawled down the cliff to the safety of Barry's lair. He knew there was a special dragon spider entrance hidden above the entrance slab in the rock cliff.

After he finished his story, he sobbed and hissed, "My poor stone Smok is being slowly hurt by Dragu's great fire bolts. The fire bolts are burning pieces of stone out of his wings. We must start the rescue mission at once!"

Agbad, Peter and Barry quickly agreed. It was decided that first thing in the morning, they would all start the perilous journey by climbing up to Dragu's castle high above them. Barry's plan was simple. After sunrise, everyone, except Peter who would be seen if he flew in daylight, would start the long climb up the cliff. No one was to fly because they could be spotted easily by Dragu's black dragons who patrolled the sky around the castle.

Barry would be their leader; Agbad, who knew the cliffs well, would scout out the climbing path. Once they reached the black rock causeway that led to the entrance of the castle, the rescue party would rest until nightfall. Then Peter and Barry would fly over to the other side of the castle and start a diversion by attacking the black dragons. The young dragons and George would then slip along the causeway and creep into the castle via an unused side door that Snip and his spies had spotted and unlocked. Bluey piped up, "Then what do we do once we get inside?"

"You creep along the main passageway which leads directly to the throne room, and there your will find your Papa Smok," Barry replied.

"And then what? How do we rescue him?" Bluey asked the question all the other members of the young rescue team also wanted to ask.

"Agbad and I will arrive – just wait and see," Barry said. They didn't miss the shadow of uncertainty that passed across his face.

The plan sounded easy, but the rescue team knew in their hearts that it wasn't.

They consoled themselves by eating a cold meal of Snark pies and gooberberry slices from Mama Draga's wicker basket. Then, finding snug places to sleep, everyone curled up to get some rest. Bluey kept thinking of his poor Papa Smok's wings being hurt by Dragu's fire bolts. He shuddered in fear and clutched his purple amulet, which glowed with warming fire. It helped to calm his racing brain.

All too soon, glimmers of dawn started to filter in through hidden window slits. Barry roused everyone and they had a quick breakfast snack from the wicker basket. Then each team member picked up their travelling packs, making sure the jars of humongous golden honey drops and boxes of Chinese checkers were all in place. With a thud, Barry threw open the door and they all filed out to face the day.

    In the growing daylight, the deep chasm seemed enormous. Bluey had to tilt his head back to see the cliff top. Without wasting a second, Agbad hopped up the rocks and started to follow a faint pathway that twisted and turned as it wound up the rock wall of the chasm. The young dragons grabbed their Tree Guard amulets and scrambled to keep up.

They were used to flying, not rock climbing. Barry was clearly at home on the snaking trail, keeping up easily, as did George, who had turned himself into a dark grey monkey that hopped and bounded up the rock face.

Bluey felt jealous, and wished for a moment that he could be Septimus – who was blissfully snoozing in his flying harness. Whisky Dog found it most difficult; his short legs made him stumble as he scrambled over rocks that the others could easily step over.

By midday they had reached about halfway. Barry ordered them to stop on a large rock ledge where they had a quick snack. This time, they had hard rolls of minced Snark that Moma Draga had made to provide them with the energy they would need for the climb. Just as they were finishing their snack, a pack of black dragons flapped overhead. Fortunately, Barry had made them crouch under an overhanging rock, so they were not spotted. The rescue team also heard the far-off high-pitched snorts and squeals of Snarks, who were hunting in the nearby forest.

After a short rest, Agbad and Barry headed off, up the rock face. Inwardly groaning, the young dragons clutched their Tree Guard amulets, and started to scramble after them. As they climbed, Bluey watched his friends flicker and fade to look like branches of shrubs or bushes they passed along the trail. He felt so thankful for Mrs K Bracken's magical gift.

The afternoon wore on, and the sun was sinking when at last the climbers saw the side of the castle's black rock

137

causeway ahead. Carefully, Agbad and Barry worked their way towards a natural rock alcove where they could hide. Above them stood two jet-black stone sentinels, one on each side of the causeway. Each had three jagged fingers, one pointing straight up, one pointing left and one pointing right. Barry explained that anyone who entered the causeway had to pass the sentinels. If they were not recognized, they would be blasted by red jets of fire.

Black dragons circled above the castle to prevent anyone flying in. Dragu believed that he was well protected. The sentinels could be safely passed by the rescue team climbing up nearer the castle entrance, away from the sentinels. Only George would be safe. He was going to fly up past the sentinels as a small bat! Barry then repeated his diversion plan: "Once the sun sets, I will fly with Agbad and Peter to start our attack at the back of the castle. That's when you must scramble up onto the causeway and run as fast as you can for the little doorway on the western side. Go in and head for Dragu's throne room as fast as you can."

Looking around, they all saw the fear glinting darkly in each other's eyes.

"Hold your special magic amulets tight," Barry commanded. They did, and everyone felt stronger and calmer.

Once the sun set, Peter silently swooped up, out of the chasm, and Agbad leapt onto his back. He then let out a bloodcurdling yell and drew his two scimitars, which flashed with blue fires. Barry unfurled his huge double wings and with an answering call that made the rocks shake, hurtled out of the chasm, straight over the top of the castle. They soon heard crashes of lightning bolts hitting rocks, and screeches of black dragons being attacked.

Bluey scrambled up the last few rocks and watched the far-off flashes that illuminated the castle battlements. The sentinels behind him seemed to be exchanging messages in flashes of blood-red fire between their outstretched fingers. The others were now standing by Bluey's side, and taking a deep breath, off they ran, as fast as their legs could carry them, towards the forbidding walls of the castle.

Reaching the end of the causeway they saw a huge iron door. It was protected by a portcullis of steel spears that seemed to be locked into the rocks at the base of the wall. Bluey realized that no one could get into the castle this way unless invited by Dragu. There, just as Barry had said, on the western side, hidden by a stone notch in the wall, was a small iron door. It was studded with small steel dwarf heads. Each head gleamed with very sharp fangs. To one side Bluey spotted a door handle the shape of a Snark head. Shuddering with fear, he pushed it. The door creaked and swung inwards, revealing a small passage that was lit by red glowworm lights. The passage seemed to lead to a much brighter chamber.

They quickly piled in, pulling the door shut. It locked itself with a loud *clang*. Now they were stuck inside Dragu's castle!

15
Dragu's throne room

Heading toward the light, clutching their glowing amulets, the rescue team crept along the dimly lit passage way. George kept his shape as a small black bat and fluttered in the lead, only stopping when he got to the entrance of the big hallway. He *squeaked*, signalling that no one could be seen.

Entering the brightly lit main passageway, Melie, remembering Barry's instructions, led the team towards the middle of the castle. No one appeared. They heard screeches, loud battle cries, and thunderous cracks of lightning bolts coming from the other side of the castle. Barry's diversion was working!

They hurried on, finally coming to a large doorway. It was painted with strange symbols that glittered and glowed with red and yellow fires. There was a large yellow door handle in the shape of a black bear's head. Bluey knew this must be the entrance to Dragu's throne room. He grabbed the handle and pushed.

The great door silently swung open to reveal a spacious multi-coloured throne room. Bluey crept in. The others followed. There, behind a black throne, was Papa Smok. His outstretched stone wings were tied back to the wall by heavy ropes. Smok's great head hung low over the throne, as if begging to be freed. Bluey's chest nearly burst with sadness. Pearls of golden tears ran down his face.

The others stood horrified at the sight of Smok. His wings looked ragged, as if something had been biting at the stone. Looking around, they saw an enormous black cauldron sitting in a corner by the fireplace, bubbling and smoking. Along a black wall were colourful banners that showed faces of great golden and Chinese dragons that Dragu had defeated in battle. The opposite wall was painted yellow and on it hung a huge mirror that reflected the faces on the banners. A domed roof of deep blue was spangled with silver stars. Behind them, next to the door, was a huge portrait of Dragu. He was prancing in a swirling red cloak, surrounded by magical creatures.

For safety, they decided that George, still in his small bat form, would fly up to a lamp high on the wall to keep watch. Melie told Whisky Dog to trot off

to sniff
around the
empty throne.
Melie and Burney
dropped their travel
packs on the flagstone floor and went to comfort Bluey.
As they did, a loud chuckle rang out and they froze as
Dragu pranced in through the doorway.

"Well, well, my little ones, come to rescue Smok have you?" he asked with a nasty grin. "How do you think you will do that?" He laughed again. It was a chuckling, evil laugh. "My dragons have beaten off your fine friends, who have fled to the dark forest licking their wounds. Now you will all be my prisoners. Maybe I can trade your sorry lives for some more treasures!"

Serious now, he pointed a glittering red claw at a pile of rope near the bubbling cauldron. The end of the rope reared up like a snake. Dragu then waved the rope towards the young dragons. Acting on his command, the rope quickly slithered over to the terrified dragons, binding them from head to toe into one big bundle. Grabbing up the roped bundle, Dragu stacked the prisoners under his victory banners. They could see Dragu prancing around in front of them as their heads were above the rope. He quickly ripped open their travel packs, pulled out the boxes of Chinese checkers and tossed them to the floor in disgust. Then he saw the jars of humongous golden honey drops, and greedily grabbed them.

"Humongous golden honey drops, so, so good for Dragu," he sang, as he wrenched the tops off all three jars. Out fell the honey drops and they flew in a golden circle around Dragu's head. His tongue darted out like a lizard as he caught and swallowed the honey drops, one by one.

With Dragu distracted by the honey drops, Mellie called Whisky Dog, who had been hiding behind the throne. Whisky bounded out, snarling and barking at Dragu. Startled, Dragu pointed a claw like an arrow, and two bolts of red fire fizzled towards Whisky Dog's head. Whisky jumped to one side, then to the other, as another fire bolt nearly hit him. A small bat then flew around Dragu's head, squeaking while diving and nipping at his ears.

Dragu's face turned redder and redder. He grabbed his middle and started to jump up and down, his face contorting as if he was in agony. He let out a gurgling screech of pain and collapsed to the floor, his eyes bulging out of his head and steam coming out of his ears.

"You have tried to poison me, but it won't work!" he rasped. Dragu slowly started to crawl on all four paws towards his bubbling cauldron.

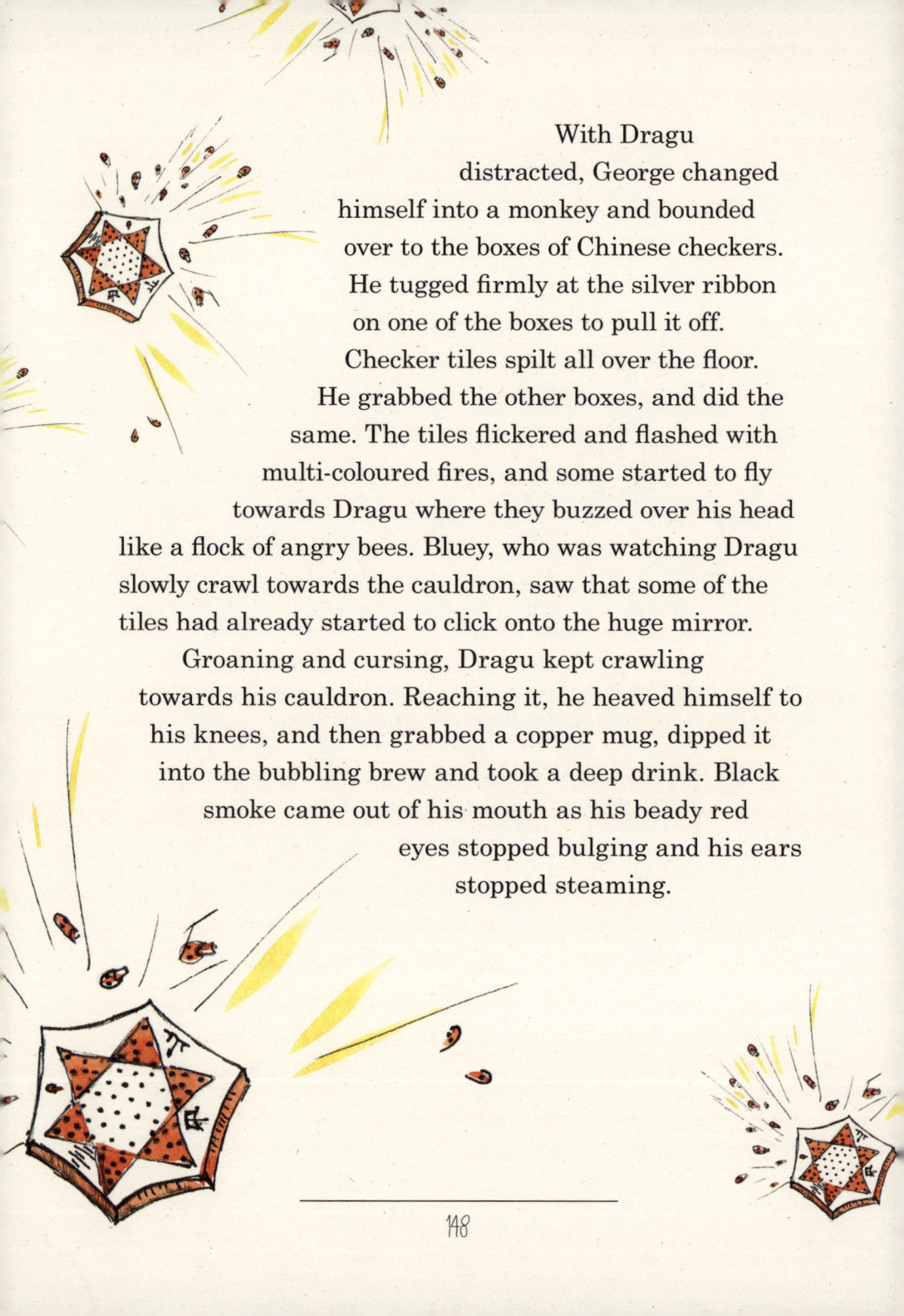

With Dragu
distracted, George changed
himself into a monkey and bounded
over to the boxes of Chinese checkers.
He tugged firmly at the silver ribbon
on one of the boxes to pull it off.
Checker tiles spilt all over the floor.
He grabbed the other boxes, and did the
same. The tiles flickered and flashed with
multi-coloured fires, and some started to fly
towards Dragu where they buzzed over his head
like a flock of angry bees. Bluey, who was watching Dragu
slowly crawl towards the cauldron, saw that some of the
tiles had already started to click onto the huge mirror.
Groaning and cursing, Dragu kept crawling
towards his cauldron. Reaching it, he heaved himself to
his knees, and then grabbed a copper mug, dipped it
into the bubbling brew and took a deep drink. Black
smoke came out of his mouth as his beady red
eyes stopped bulging and his ears
stopped steaming.

Standing to his full height and snarling curses, Dragu turned around, muttered a healing spell and started to move towards the terrified young dragons. The room was now abuzz with Chinese checkers flying everywhere. Many circled around Dragu's head. Others flew to the mirror, and with a steady *click, click, click*, stuck to its edges. As Dragu batted the checkers away from his angry face, they too were drawn to the mirror where they stuck.

Whisky Dog had backed behind the black throne out of harm's way. That left George, who dodged the red fire bolts that Dragu was firing at him. Still in his monkey shape, George picked up a checkerboard to use it as a shield, but realized that a flimsy board would not stop bolts of fire.

Dragu had nearly reached his prisoners when, in desperation, George hurled the board straight at Dragu's head. It sliced through the air like a spinning dinner plate, hit Dragu's red turban and knocked it off his head. Startled, Dragu howled in anger like a wounded Snark. He turned and ran towards George, trying to catch him. George bounded back towards the throne, as if to hide. But instead, turned himself into a large green gecko, and using his now sticky feet, he skittled up the wall and onto the blue spangled ceiling.

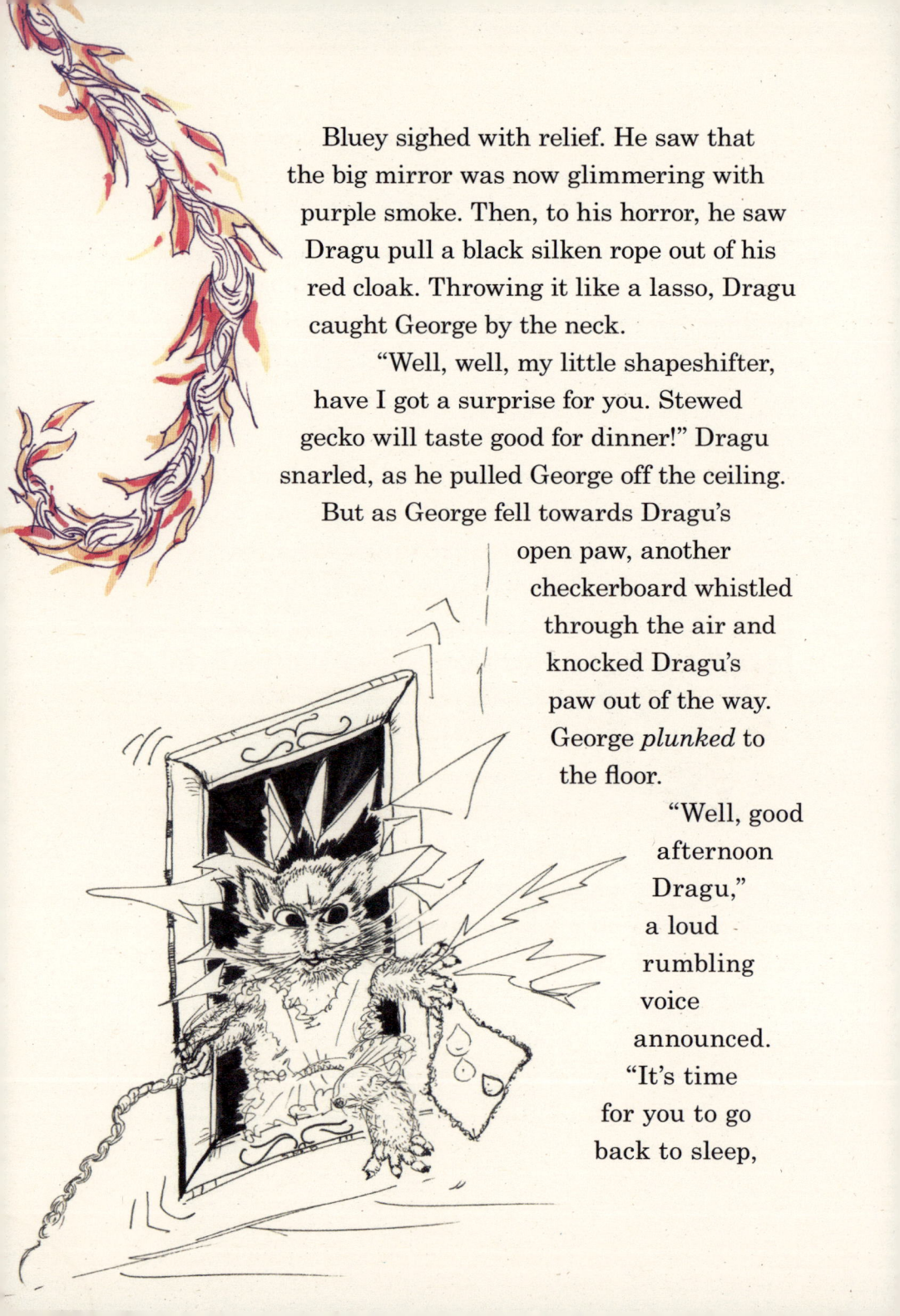

Bluey sighed with relief. He saw that the big mirror was now glimmering with purple smoke. Then, to his horror, he saw Dragu pull a black silken rope out of his red cloak. Throwing it like a lasso, Dragu caught George by the neck.

"Well, well, my little shapeshifter, have I got a surprise for you. Stewed gecko will taste good for dinner!" Dragu snarled, as he pulled George off the ceiling. But as George fell towards Dragu's open paw, another checkerboard whistled through the air and knocked Dragu's paw out of the way. George *plunked* to the floor.

"Well, good afternoon Dragu," a loud rumbling voice announced. "It's time for you to go back to sleep, forever this time!" Uncle Chin seemed to have appeared from nowhere. His skilful aim with the checkerboard had just saved George's life.

Dragu whirled around in surprise. He saw Uncle Chin, Mrs P Hamster and Auntie Lulu standing by, what was now, an inky-black mirror. Uncle Chin's silver eyebrow lightning was jumping off his face. Auntie Lulu, standing beside him, was holding an armful of what looked like silver balloons, full of swirling blue water. Mrs P Hamster was holding out her purple kerchief, which was folded like a pointed dagger.

Dragu grabbed the big red amulet that hung on a golden chain around his neck, and roared in anger. "You can't capture me. I am far stronger. Now I will capture you all, cook you in my cauldron and eat your bones!"

As Dragu started to scream a spell, coloured ropes of flame, one of fiery purple and one ice-cold silver, sprang out and wrapped themselves around Dragu's paws, pulling them away from the amulet. Mrs P Hamster's kerchief crackled with energy as her purple rope flamed. It started to burn Dragu. Uncle Chin was humming a high-pitched spell in a strange language. His silver rope turned into, what looked to Bluey to be, sparkling ice-blue water. It started to freeze Dragu, whose burning fur was giving off blue smoke.

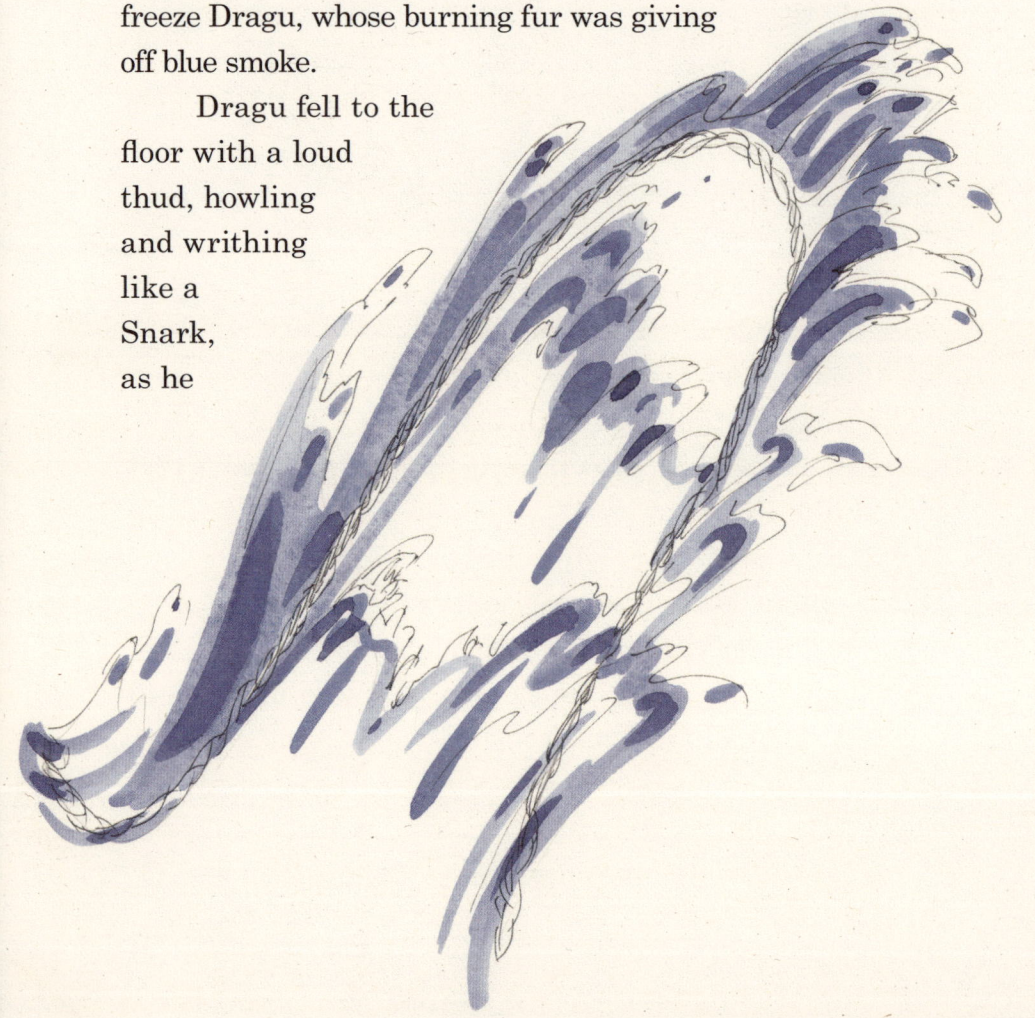

Dragu fell to the floor with a loud thud, howling and writhing like a Snark, as he thrashed his paws around, trying to fight off the two burning and freezing magic ropes.

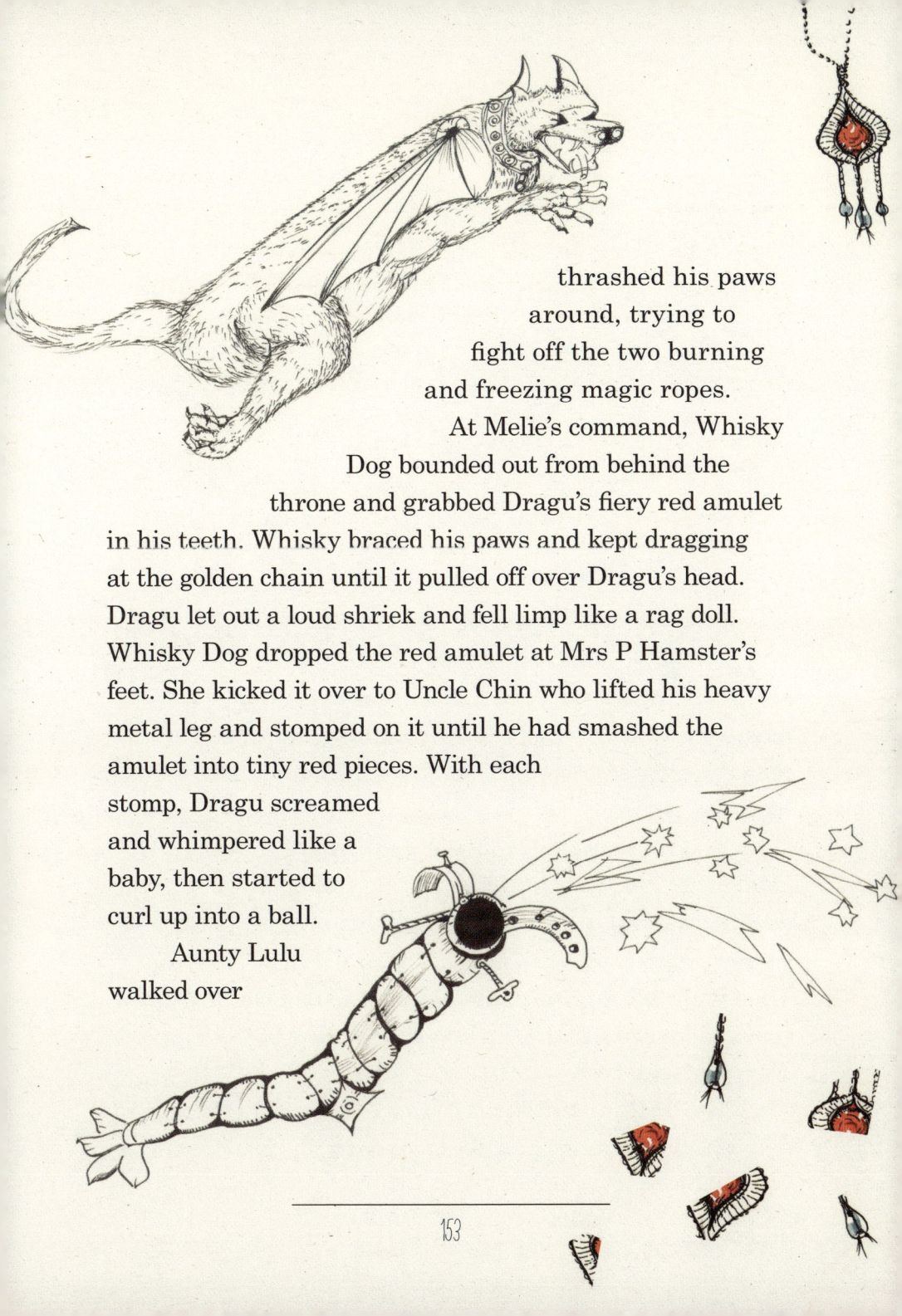

At Melie's command, Whisky Dog bounded out from behind the throne and grabbed Dragu's fiery red amulet in his teeth. Whisky braced his paws and kept dragging at the golden chain until it pulled off over Dragu's head. Dragu let out a loud shriek and fell limp like a rag doll. Whisky Dog dropped the red amulet at Mrs P Hamster's feet. She kicked it over to Uncle Chin who lifted his heavy metal leg and stomped on it until he had smashed the amulet into tiny red pieces. With each stomp, Dragu screamed and whimpered like a baby, then started to curl up into a ball.

Aunty Lulu walked over

to Dragu. She dropped
the blue water balloons
onto his twitching body.

Mrs P Hamster and Uncle Chin released their magic ropes as Aunty Lulu cast an ice-spell that made the water stick to Dragu, freezing him into a big blue block of ice.

Then both Mrs P Hamster and Uncle Chin chanted loudly together to cast an Everlasting Holdall spell over the now frozen Dragu. As they continued to chant, the block of ice started to spin into the air. Faster and faster it spun. Then it spiralled towards the ceiling where a thick black cloud had formed and, with a loud echoing *FLOOMP*, it disappeared.

Mrs P Hamster hurried over to the young dragons who wanted to jump up and down with joy, but couldn't.

She waved her purple kerchief and the magic rope untied itself and slithered back into its corner.

A shaken George reappeared and rushed to Aunty Lulu. Meanwhile, Whisky Dog bounded over to lick the golden tears from Bluey's face. The rescue team cheered and started to talk all at once, wanting to know exactly how they had been saved. And most importantly, where had Dragu gone?

Smiling, Mrs P Hamster told them that Dragu's blue ice block was now safely locked away, deep in a dark cave at the top of the highest mountain in Transylvania. Uncle Chin explained that the only way to get himself, Aunty Lulu, and Mrs P Hamster into Dragu's castle was through the magic mirror. To do this, he admitted, they had decided to send in the young rescue team, knowing that they would be captured. He knew that the checkers, once released, would turn the mirror into a portal to let them in. They were confident the plan would work and, fortunately, it had. But now, much more difficult, was the question, how to free Smok?

Barry Basilisk

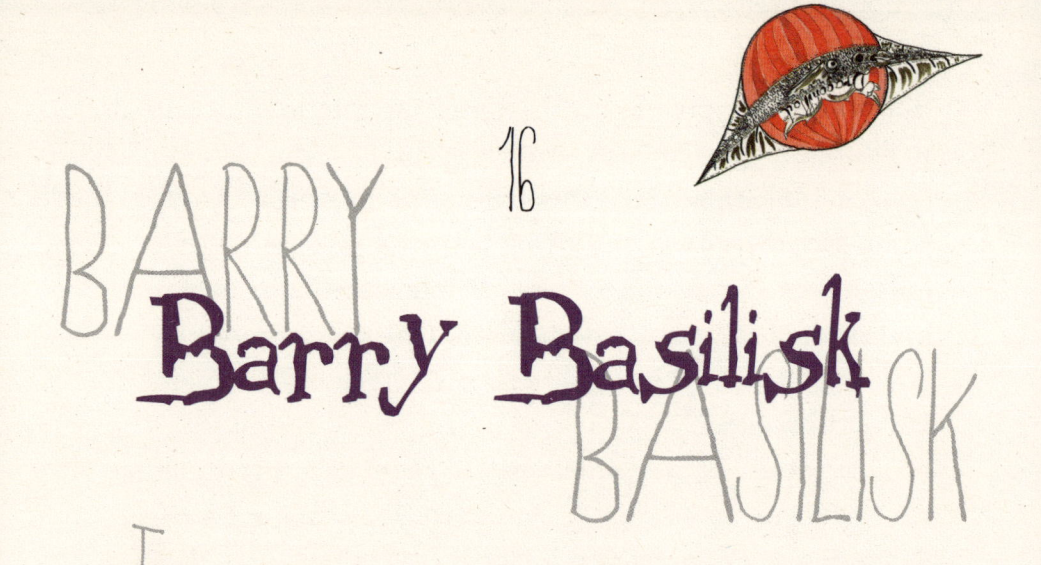

The rescue team's joy stopped as Mrs P Hamster and Uncle Chin swung around to watch the door. In the distance they heard a very loud metal scraping, followed by a clang of huge iron doors swinging open. Someone had opened the portcullis and doors to the castle. A loud stomping in the main hallway could be heard; this was followed by the clatter of bronze hooves, and everyone relaxed.

Into the throne room stomped Barry Basilisk, Peter Pegasus and a tired looking Agbad. Loud clapping and cheering erupted, especially from George and the young dragons. They had believed Dragu when he told them that Barry and his two companions had fled to the forest defeated.

"What a wonderful fight we had," exclaimed Barry. "I have not had so much fun since I left this castle for the Blue Tier."

Bluey blurted out, "You were *here*?"

"Why, yes, young Bluey. I was the Grand Master of this castle and all of Transylvania before I duelled with a great golden dragon called Sebastian the Bold. We fought tooth and nail for weeks, burning forests, dwarfs and goblins in our way. A pack of Chinese dragons tried to stop us, but we battled on. Until one day your Uncle Chin, who had already lost a leg in the fight, bravely came to me with a peace plan. He suggested that, instead of burning everything and causing much devastation, we try living a peaceful life in a far-off land full of gooberberries and Snarks to munch. I love gooberberries and Snark pies, so I agreed to see what the Blue Tier was like." He suddenly stopped, looking very sad.

"But what happened to Sebastian the Bold?" Bluey asked.

"Well, one of my thunder bolts had mortally hurt Sebastian, and his dragon fire was slowly going out. Sebastian and I agreed to stop fighting and he decided to come with me to the Blue Tier. I found my new lair at Skeleton Point. The Red Rock cliffs, with the roaring silver-blue sea at our feet, was a perfect place for Sebastian to sit in the sunlight. We became great friends and then, one morning, I came out of my lair to find that Sebastian had turned into a rock dragon. I was terribly sad and tried, but I failed to bring him back to life. At least he is always there with me."

Hearing this, Bluey wondered how could Barry save Papa Smok if he could not save Sebastian. His heart sank.

Seeing the look on Bluey's face, Barry went on, "Don't you worry. Yes, your Papa Smok is now a rock dragon. But, together with your Uncle Chin and Mrs P Hamster's magical power, we will turn him back into a real golden dragon!"

Barry turned to Agbad and asked him to shut the portcullis and castle doors so that no black dragons or Snarks could sneak in to attack them. He then asked Mrs P Hamster to summon Moma Draga from the Blue Tier. "Poor Smok, he will want to see his family," Barry said, "and seeing your Moma Draga will give him strength to recover."

To the young dragons, he said, "Now Bluey, you and the others are to go to the castle kitchen. Just follow the main passageway and you will find it. I want you to find as many pots and buckets as you can carry, and bring them back and fill them from Dragu's cauldron. Aunty Lulu will cast a healing spell over the cauldron water, and as I cast my spell on Smok, you will all splash the magic water on his wings. It will help heal them."

Barry had a task for Peter. "I want you to breath cold white starlight onto Smok's head when I start my spell," he directed. "It will soothe his pain as he turns from stone into a golden dragon again."

The young dragons and George rushed off to find the castle kitchen. Up the great hallway they ran, and soon found a black door that opened into a big kitchen. A roaring fire glowed in the hearth and all sorts of pots, pans and copper basins hung from hooks on the walls. Each of them grabbed two things to fill with cauldron water to throw. Bluey looked for the biggest copper basins he could carry, as he knew that Papa Smok's wings would need lots of magic healing water. Even Whisky Dog grabbed a copper scoop in his teeth to drag back to the throne room.

     Soon everyone had returned to the throne room. Barry stomped over to the black stone throne and, with a mighty heave, ripped it up from the floor. He swung it high over his head and smashed it onto the floor where it shattered into a heap of tiny pieces. There, sticking out of the pile was a large black metal box covered in fiery red runes. As Barry picked up the box, the runes smoked and curled around Barry's great head.

     Barry tapped the top with both claws and muttered a spell. The heavy lid flew open. He reached in and pulled out a black amulet with a mirrored face that gleamed with small blue stars. Barry put it over his head, and the amulet came to life. It pulsed with small bolts of blue lightning. Barry unfurled his great double wings and spread them out. They almost touched each wall of the room. Then Barry's wings glowed and pulsed with the same liquid blue lightning that had appeared on the flight to Transylvania.

Aunty Lulu finished her healing spell and Barry ordered the young dragons and George to start throwing cauldron water on Smok's outstretched wings. Whisky Dog helped by swooping into the cauldron with his scoop and dropping water onto Smok's wingtips. As they all did this, the water seemed to soak into the stone and, rather than drip off, it gave off smoky-white steam. With rising excitement, everyone saw that the pits and cracks in Smok's ragged stone wings had started to heal. George and the young dragons redoubled their efforts and threw more and more water at Smok.

Their arms were starting to tire when they heard a shrill scream behind them. They spun round and saw Moma Draga, her face contorted in anguish. She had just stepped out from the magic mirror, and her first sight was of a smoking Smok being doused in water. Barry hastily explained that he was not on fire but being brought back to life, and invited her to join in throwing water. She grabbed one of Bluey's pots and ran to the cauldron.

Barry then asked Uncle Chin and Mrs P Hamster to prepare to cast spells to release the ropes that held Smok's wings that were pinned to the rock wall behind him. They moved to stand on either side of Barry. Once more, a purple rope appeared from Mrs P Hamster's kerchief and a silver-blue rope shot from Uncle Chin's outstretched claw. This time the magic ropes were cool as they snaked and swirled above Smok's pinned wings.

Stepping close to Smok's face, Barry began to chant a spell in an unearthly deep tone. It sounded to Bluey like the groaning of huge rocks rubbing together deep in the earth. Barry's blue fires pulsed bright and small bolts of lightning kept running around the edges of his wings. Lifting a huge black claw, Barry pointed at Smok's forehead. A bolt of red-black fire started to lick around Smok's head. Peter joined in to huff a stream of cold silver starlight at Smok's head.

Barry's fire seemed to be alive, as it crept from Smok's head, down over his stony scales and out over his outstretched stone wings. As the fire crept over Smok's stone body it looked as if he was covered in swirling red-black smoke. Smok's body appeared to be drinking in the black fire and, as it did so, the stone heated up. The heat grew and grew, finally making the water that was being hurled over him, start to hiss with steam.

Barry took a deep breath, renewing his efforts, but his wings started to droop, and all the blue fires disappeared. But just as Barry tired, Smok's whole body started to return to its normal golden colour. Blue smoke started to come

162

out of his mouth. Barry moaned in pain, then grunted "Now!" and both the purple and silver blue magic ropes, snapping as if they were alive, wrapped themselves over Smok's wings.

The anxious watchers heard loud snaps as Dragu's ropes that bound Smok's wings finally burnt off. Smok's eyes flicked open, he staggered, let out a smoky breath, folded his wings and sank to the floor with a thud. Moma Draga hooted in delight and rushed over to embrace him. Everyone else was staring in horror at Barry.

Barry stood silent now, like a huge black gargoyle. His double wings were folded down over his back and his great claws hung limply by his side. More horrifying was the sound of a slow *clink, clink*, as small pieces of black scales fell from Barry's body. With a loud

Boom!

his now empty amulet shattered into a thousand pieces and fell at his feet. Its black iron chain clanged to the floor. Then Barry's whole body dissolved into tiny pieces of ashes that looked as if they had come out of a furnace. Soon, all that was left of Barry was a heap of black ashes.

Everyone stood horrified at the sight of the ash pile. Only Uncle Chin reacted. He dug out a large leather pouch from his hollow leg and handed it to Bluey. "Take this pouch, and with the help of your friends, sweep up every bit of Barry. We must take him back to the Blue Tier as soon as possible."

Looking grim, Mrs P Hamster produced purple hand brooms and small scoops for each young dragon and one for George. Bluey had been so happy to see his Papa Smok restored to life, but now he did not know whether to laugh or cry. His Papa Smok was safe in Moma Draga's arms; Dragu had been defeated and banished. Yet, here was one of his best friends tuned into a heap of ashes at his feet!

Looking up, Bluey saw Uncle Chin and Mrs P Hamster talking and Agbad and Peter walking over to join them. They all looked serious. What were they planning? The dragon spiders were sitting still in shock. Whisky Dog lay nearby, looking sad with his head on his paws.

Carefully following Uncle Chin's command, Bluey, Burney, Melie and George swept up Barry's ashes. Bluey felt that there could be no celebration of Dragu's defeat with Barry gone.

They soon finished their sad task and Uncle Chin called them over. Looking very stern he said, "With Barry gone we are not safe any longer. The black dragons will soon find out he is not here, and they will attack us. So, this is what we will do. First, I'll have Moma Draga take Papa Smok back to the Blue Tier. Agbad must ride with Peter and use the blue lightning to get home. Aunty Lulu, Mrs P Hamster, and I will travel back through the magic mirror. You young dragons and George will be transported home the same way. The mirror will be destroyed after we pass through so no one can follow us. Now Bluey, as Barry was your special friend, it will be your task to carry the pouch of his ashes home to his lair. We will all meet at the Purple Possum tomorrow, to plan Barry's burial."

Papa Smok was still weak. He was now able to walk, slowly at first, then more quickly, around the throne room where he flexed his great wings. His red dragon fire was getting stronger by the minute. Moma Draga followed him, holding one of his claws to help steady him, as he wobbled on his feet. Each time they passed Dragu's cauldron, Smok took a great gulp of Auntie Lulu's healing water. Everybody else gathered their things and prepared to leave. The dragon spiders and Whisky Dog jumped into their flying harnesses.

Bluey watched Moma Draga draw a magic circle on the floor. A yellow fire flared and started to generate a huge black cloud, which slid down over her golden body that supported a smiling Smok. There was a clap of thunder and a big flash of red lightning, a now familiar *FLOOMP*, and the cloud disappeared with Moma Draga and Smok in it. Agbad leapt onto Peter's broad back. Peter's bronze hooves clanged as he cantered off down the main passageway to fly home.

Bluey clutched the black pouch of Barry's ashes. He, George, and the other young dragons followed Auntie Lulu and Mrs P Hamster over to the magic mirror. The surface of the mirror was still inky-black, but it flickered with small dots of silver starlight. Uncle Chin told the youngsters to watch Auntie Lulu jump straight into the mirror and then do the same when their turn came.

Bluey watched bug-eyed, as Auntie Lulu appeared to melt into the black surface of the mirror without making a ripple. Mrs P Hamster did the same, but as she disappeared a paw appeared beckoning Bluey to follow. Taking a deep breath, he jumped. Everything disappeared. Opening his eyes, there was nothing to see, not even a tiny twinkle of starlight, just pitch-blackness. He felt as if he was being turned inside out and twisted around at the same time. His body seemed as light as a feather as it floated in a dark space that buzzed with powerful magical energy.

17

Sebastian the Bold

After what seemed only a few minutes, Bluey tumbled out of the Purple Possum hall mirror, with George and the other dragons right behind. Mrs P Hamster reached out, grabbed him by the claw saying, "Quickly now, into the living room. The others are waiting."

There, standing gazing into each other's golden eyes, were Moma Draga and Papa Smok, still holding claws. Auntie Lulu was putting the silver chains back on the magic chest. Bluey rushed over to hug Papa Smok. His heart jumped with joy at the thought of Smok taking him Snark hunting and then getting home to the lair, sharing celebration snacks of gooberberry slices that Moma Draga would have waiting for them.

Just then, Agbad swooped in on Peter's back – both looking for all the world as though they had just been out for an afternoon's Snark hunt. Soon everyone, except Uncle Chin, had arrived.

Suddenly, a loud bang echoed from the hallway, accompanied by the tinkle of breaking glass. Bluey peered out to see Uncle Chin wiping bits of the hall mirror off his hollow leg.

"The deed is done. The mirror in Dragu's throne room is shattered, so we don't have to worry about attack from that direction!"

Still holding the black pouch of Barry's ashes, Bluey asked Uncle Chin, "What do we do now? How do we bury Barry?" More golden tears ran down his face, and his heart was heavy.

Uncle Chin looked at Bluey's teary face and decided that plans for Barry's burial had to be made now. Gathering everybody in the living room he told them, "Tomorrow at sundown we will gather at Skeleton Point by Dragon Rock. There, with Bluey's help, we will pour Barry's ashes into the sea. Sam will lead the dragon spiders in a battle song, and we will bid Barry goodbye. Then we will return to the Purple Possum to celebrate the defeat of Dragu, with basket loads of gooberberry slices, minced Snark pies and Mrs P Hamster's famous purple soda! Now, everyone off to your lairs, and get some well-earned rest until we meet at Dragon Rock."

The dragon spiders hooted at the thought of the coming feast; but Bluey just felt sad.

Bluey and Burney said goodbye to everyone, and flew with Moma Draga and Papa Smok back to their lair on the Blue Tier. Bluey wanted to feel only happiness to have his beloved Papa Smok home, but holding the pouch of Barry's ashes made him feel miserable.

When they got back to the lair, Moma Draga gave Bluey a big hug. She knew how sad he was to lose his friend Barry and she tried to make him feel better by offering him an extra slice of gooberberry pie. It didn't help. He crawled into his bunk that night and thought of all the wonderful times he had spent with Barry. His sleep was haunted by the vision of Barry crumbling into ashes as Papa Smok came back to life.

Next morning Bluey just wanted to stay home in the snug lair. Moma Draga flapped off to the Purple Possum to help prepare the celebration feast. Papa Smok went around to see Uncle Chin. They needed to talk about the resistance in Transylvania. Burney flew off to find George and Wart Nose.

Bluey thought he would be alone. Then he heard a knock on the door, and in walked Melie with Whisky Dog, George, Burney and Wart Nose. They tried to cheer him up. Nothing worked, not even George turning himself into a big blue balloon that bounced around, looking like it had a frozen Dragu trapped inside. As the afternoon wore on Bluey felt even more miserable. He just kept thinking about having to pour Barry's ashes into the sea.

As the sun started to set they got ready and flapped off to Skeleton Point. Landing by the entrance to Barry's lair, they saw that everyone had already arrived. Bluey saw Uncle Chin and Auntie Lulu carrying big Chinese rockets. Mrs P Hamster had set up a large bronze dragon gong on a tripod next to the crouching rock body of Sebastian the Bold.

Gazing up at the huge stone dragon, Bluey saw a cloud of yellow and black butterflies circling its head. Sun shone through the butterflies' wings, making them look like a yellow and black circlet of gold swirling around Sebastian's head. Silver-flecked blue waves gently lapped against the rocks below. Bluey also noticed some small thunderclouds popping up on the horizon.

Uncle Chin let off a couple of small red rockets and called everyone to gather at the base of Dragon Rock. He told Bluey to climb up onto Sebastian's head and, at the signal of his big rockets, he was to open the pouch and pour Barry's ashes into the sea below.

Stepping up onto a rock that rested against Sebastian's side, Uncle Chin called for silence and began to tell Barry's story. That Barry had been the strongest Basilisk ever, the Grand Master of Transylvania, who had lived in the big Castle they now all knew. He talked of the fighting that took place between the golden dragons and Barry who, in those days, commanded the black dragons. He told them how Barry had finally retired to the Blue Tier, having made good friends with his former enemy, Sebastian the Bold, and that when Barry left his castle it had been taken over by Dragu. He said that, sadly, Dragu had found powerful magic, which came from an enchanted amulet he had captured on a hunting raid at Uncle Chin's old Chinese dragon lair in the far-off Moon Mountains.

Bluey listened transfixed. The sun disappeared behind a cloud. Looking up, Bluey saw that one of the thunderclouds was directly overhead. Strangely, the cloud was glowing with red and blue lightning bolts but there was no thunder. "How odd," thought Bluey. There was a short silence and Bluey realized that Uncle Chin had finished his story. Everyone started to clap, accompanied by the lapping and gurgling of the sea against the rocks. Bluey shuddered at what he had to do now.

Mrs P Hamster picked up a wooden hammer, which had a purple scarf tied around its handle. She walked over to the bronze dragon gong. Uncle Chin bent down and fired off two enormous rockets that flew straight up and exploded in the thundercloud. As they boomed above, he pointed his claw at Bluey and called out, "Now, Bluey!"

Shaking and crying with grief, Bluey picked up the black pouch and untied its top. He lifted it up, ready to empty the ashes over Sebastian's head. As he did so, Mrs P Hamster hit the gong hard. It reverberated with an unearthly *bong, bong, bong*, like a set of big bronze cymbals. Overhead there were multiple blue bolts of lightning followed by huge cracks of thunder. Bluey felt the rock under his feet shift and he nearly fell over as Sebastian seemed to stir and shake his great head. Hail and rain pelted out of the sky, causing Bluey to lose his grip and drop the bag of Barry's ashes. As he made a grab for the bag, it split open and he watched as the ashes were washed down into Sebastian's now wide-open mouth.

    The rain stopped just as fast as it had started, and the small thundercloud scudded away in a sudden breeze. The last rays of the setting sun were shining directly on Sebastian's head. Bluey saw Uncle Chin pointing a silver claw at a curl of black smoke that was coming out of Sebastian's mouth. The smoke thickened and rose above Bluey's head, swirling like butterflies.

    Slowly the smoke formed a solid black rope that twisted around and around itself. Bluey thought of dancing black snakes gathering in the air. He watched as the smoke continued to flow from Sebastian's mouth. Soon the smoke petered out and stopped. When it did so, Sebastian's mouth snapped shut and Bluey felt him settle back into his rock dragon form again.

    Fed by the last of the smoke from Sebastian's mouth, the twisting smoke cloud got bigger and familiar blue lightning flashes started to run around its edges. As Bluey watched the cloud grow, Mrs P Hamster hit the dragon gong again and again.

Its reverberations echoed across the rocks and up into the smoke cloud.

The inky-black cloud shook with the reverberations for a few minutes. Then, with another bright flash of blue light, it started to take on a familiar shape. The shape kept growing. It sprouted big double wings and then a long thick serpent's tail, followed by big arms with huge claws, and finally, an eagle's head appeared. It looked for all the world like Barry.

With mounting excitement Bluey saw that, yes, it was his old Basilisk friend! Barry was hovering above them with his great double wings gently flapping as they flashed with familiar blue lightning. His wings were now spread out over the amazed crowd like a sheltering umbrella.

Grinning, Barry landed behind Bluey, bent down and patted Sebastian on his stone back. "Well, well, my old friend, you still have some powerful magic left in your heart." Then, bowing to Mrs P Hamster and Uncle Chin, he formally thanked them for bringing him home.

Everyone yelled and cheered in joy. The dragon spiders hooted and stomped their iron feet. Bluey rushed over to Barry and gave him a great big hug. Uncle Chin fired off the rest of his rockets, lighting up the sea for miles around with whistling sparkles of coloured lights.

To get everyone's attention, Mrs P Hamster struck her bronze gong one more time and happily announced that a victory celebration was about to start at the Purple Possum. Barry grabbed Bluey by the claw and gleefully called out to the crowd, "I am *very* hungry. There are gooberberry pies, hot minced Snark pies and bottles of purple lemonade waiting. Follow me!"

He leapt into the air, followed by a happy, singing crowd.

The end END

OFF TO THE PARTY

This is tanned Snark Skin

Acknowledgements

To Sue Briginshaw, my illustrator, whose drawings helped liberate the storytelling. Her superb depictions capture Bluey's story just as I had envisioned it.

To Pamela Burton, who encouraged me to write, challenged me to use my imagination, and helped with the editing.

To Melie, Sam and George whose youthful commentary and suggestions contributed to Bluey and his friends' magical adventures!

To Robin Gibson for her generosity in giving her time to edit and comment on my first draft.

My thanks also to Don Defenderfer, Kent Whitmore and Lucinda Sharp for the production of this book.

Text copyright © 2018 Ken Mackay
Illustrations copyright © 2018 Sue Briginshaw

ISBN 978-0-6483631-6-3

All rights reserved. Without limiting the rights under copyright above, no part of this publication may be reproduced, stored or introduced into a retrieval system, or transmitted in any form or by any means (electronic, mechanical, photocopying, recording or otherwise), without prior written permission of the copyright holders.

Published by Forty South Pty Ltd
fortysouth.com.au

Printed by Choice Printing Group
choiceprintgroup.com

Orb, little Orb
You have travelled so far!
Zip Through the red heat of Dragon Fire
And iCy cold of Black Night Air

Zip

Zip